Classic Knits

A handy step-by-step guide

DK

LONDON, NEW YORK, MELBOURNE,
MUNICH, DELHI

Project Editor Katharine Goddard
Senior Art Editors Elaine Hewson
Managing Editor Penny Smith
Senior Managing Art Editor Marianne Markham
Producer, Pre-Production Rebecca Fallowfield
Senior Producer Katherine Whyte
Special Sales Creative Project Manager Alison Donovan

DK INDIA
Editors Janashree Singha, Manasvi Vohra
Senior Art Editor Balwant Singh
Art Editor Zaurin Thoidingjam
Assistant Art Editor Nikita Sodhi
DTP Designer Satish Chandra Gaur

First published in Great Britain in 2014
by Dorling Kindersley Limited
80 Strand, London WC2R 0RL

Material in this publication was previously published in:
Big Book of Knitting (2013)

A Penguin Random House Company

Copyright © 2013, 2014
Dorling Kindersley Limited

2 4 6 8 10 9 7 5 3 1
001 – 193362 – Jun/2014

This edition produced for The Book People Ltd,
Hall Wood Avenue, Haydock, St Helens, WA11 9UL

A CIP catalogue record for this book is available
from the British Library

ISBN 978-1-4093-6969-1

Printed and bound in China by Leo Paper Products Ltd.

Discover more at **www.dk.com/crafts**

Contents

Introduction

This book is suitable for all knitters, whether you have never held a pair of needles before or are an experienced knitter. All key areas are covered – with over 25 patterns, plus tools and materials, and techniques. The Techniques chapter features a vast array of techniques, from simply understanding a pattern to more complicated cables, lace knitting and colourwork. With *Classic Knits* you'll find everything you need to knit with accuracy, confidence, and flair.

The Clothes and accessories chapter contains patterns for a range of skill levels and a variety of techniques. Here you can bring your skills to fruition, knitting garments for all the family, plus a choice of accessories. The children's clothes are given in three sizes, specified by age, while the Men's sleeveless pullover includes four sizes – small, medium, large, and extra large.

Each project shows the yarn and stitch tension used, but if you substitute a yarn refer to p.11 for equivalent standard yarn weights from which to choose. Select one that has the same stitch and row count on the ballband as that in the pattern, and always work a tension swatch (see p.15). Adjust your needle size if necessary to achieve the correct stitch tension so that your project comes out at the correct size. Check that the tension swatch in the new yarn looks and feels suitable for the project. Calculate the amount of yarn by yardage/meterage, as the amount needed may vary.

Yarns

A yarn is the long, stranded, spun fibre that we knit with. There are many types of yarns, allowing knitters to enjoy a variety of sensory experiences as they express themselves through the medium. Yarns may be made of different fibres and have a range of textures. Their possibilities are exciting: you can, in theory, knit with anything – from a skein of supple silk sock yarn to the plastic bag that you brought it home in. Choose from a colour palette that sweeps from subtle, muted tones to eye-popping brights.

Wool The hair, or wool, of a variety of breeds of sheep, such as the Shetland Moorit or Bluefaced Leicester, is made into pure wool yarns, or blended with other fibres. It is very warm and hard-wearing, and great for winter wear such as jackets, cardigans, hats, and gloves. Some wool is rough, but it will soften with wear and washing. Wool sold as "organic" often contains a high proportion of lanolin, making a strong, waterproof yarn.

Merino wool This is wool from the merino sheep, which is said to have one of the softest wools of any sheep breed. The bouncy, smooth-surfaced fibre is just as warm as a more wiry, coarse wool. Merino is a fantastic choice for wearing against the skin, and is often treated to make it suitable for machine-washing. Good for soft scarves, arm warmers, and children's garments.

Alpaca This fibre has a luxurious feel and is one of the warmest natural fibres you can knit with. Even a fine, 4-ply garment provides sufficient insulation in bitterly cold weather. The alpaca is related to the llama. Alpaca yarn is perfect for ski hats, and thick, cosy jumpers and socks. You will also find baby alpaca yarn available, which is softer still.

Mohair This fibre is the hair of the angora goat, and it produces a unique natural "halo" when knitted up. Working with it is quite challenging, as its frizzy appearance makes it difficult to see the structure of the knitting and any mistakes made. Mohair makes particularly interesting oversized jumpers or accessories. It is not advisable to use it for babywear as it may shed hair when newly made, which could be dangerous if inhaled.

Wool

Merino wool

Alpaca

Mohair

Bamboo

Cashmere

Matt cotton

Silk

Linen

Bamboo Modern technology has enabled us to derive flexible fibres from the inside of rigid, brittle bamboo canes. Bamboo fibre is a super sleek imitation of silk fibre, and is made into a floppy and airy yarn that is ideal for lightweight shrugs and shawls.

Cashmere This fibre is the hair from a goat, which makes an ultra-luxurious, velvety-soft yarn. It is light but incredibly strong, and weighs very little by the metre; it often goes further than a pure wool or cotton. It is expensive to produce and is often blended with other fibres in a yarn to add softness. Cashmere should be enjoyed close to the skin in scarves, snoods, or sweaters. Treat it with great care; finished items may be dry-clean only.

Matt cotton Cotton is the fluffy mass that grows around the seeds of the cotton plant. It is spun into a breathable, summery fibre. Most cotton yarns are easy to wash, and when cared for correctly, can be incredibly robust and last for decades. It is therefore a good fibre for homewares, knitted pouches, and shoulder bags. Pure, untreated cotton is ideal for hand-dyeing.

Silk The silkworm, a caterpillar that eats mulberry leaves, spins a cocoon in order to develop into a moth. It is from the fibres of the cocoon that silk is made. Silk is shiny and sleek, very delicate, and owing to its extraordinary source, very expensive. The luxurious texture of silk yarn makes it ideal for wedding and christening gifts, and indulgent fitted knitwear.

Linen This fibre is commonly derived from the flax plant. It is rather wiry, with an oily, waxy surface, but blossoms into a sleek, soft, breathable yarn that is ideal for knitting into lightweight cardigans and tops to wear in warm weather.

Yarn weights

The yarn "weight" refers to the thickness of a yarn. Some yarns are spun by manufacturers to fall into what are considered as "standard" yarn weights, such as UK double-knitting and aran, and US sport or worsted. These standard weights have long histories and will probably be around for some time to come. However, even within these standard weights there is slight variation in thickness, and textured novelty yarns are not easy to categorize by thickness alone.

Visual yarn thickness is only one indicator of a yarn-weight category. A yarn can look thicker than another yarn purely because of its loft, the air between the fibres, and the springiness of the strands. By pulling a strand between your hands you can see how much loft it has by how much the thickness diminishes when the yarn is stretched. The ply of a yarn is also not an indication of yarn thickness. Plies are the strands spun together around each other to form the yarn. A yarn with four plies can be very thick or very thin depending on the thickness of each individual ply.

In order to help knitters attempting to match like for like when looking for a substitute yarn for their knitting pattern, yarn manufacturers have created a table of yarn weights. This table (opposite) demonstrates how to find the nearest yarn substitute if you are unable to purchase the yarn specified in a knitting pattern. The very best indication of a yarn weight is the manufacturer's recommended tension and needle size for the yarn. (These will produce a knitted fabric that is loose enough to be soft and flexible but not so loose that it loses its shape.) Two yarns with the same fibre content and the same recommended tension and needle size will be ideal substitutes for each other.

TOP TIP

A ply is a single twisted strand – the more plies, the thicker the yarn.

Yarn labels

Yarn is usually packaged with a label that provides all the information you need to knit successfully. Before you buy, always read the label carefully to establish the type of yarn, suggested needle size, care instructions, and ball length.

Decide whether you require an easy-care yarn and check the care instructions. Fibre content will indicate whether the yarn is synthetic, natural, or a mix of fibres. The ball length will enable you to calculate how many balls are required especially when substituting yarn. Check the dye lot number if you are purchasing several balls, as variations in colour can occur across different dye lots.

Lace/2-ply Extremely light and often sold in a plentiful quantity. If worked on needles of the recommended size, the yarn produces a very fine-knit, delicate result. It can be more pleasurable to use the yarn with slightly larger needles for a more open fabric and a quicker knit.

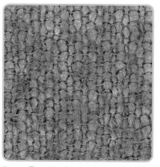

Superfine/3-ply An ideal choice for lightweight lace work. It goes a long way per ball, and requires very slim needles. A gossamer yarn such as this one (above) highlights stitch definition and fine detail, which is why intricate lace work looks stunning in superfine yarn.

Fine/4-ply Many knitters prefer fine to superfine yarn as it uses a more comfortable needle size yet still produces a lightweight knit. It is ideal for socks and baby clothes. The small stitches and neat appearance also suit delicate texture and colourwork items.

Standard yarn weight chart

Yarn symbol		**0** Lace	**1** Superfine	**2** Fine	**3** Light	**4** Medium	**5** Bulky	**6** Super bulky
Recommended needle sizes	Metric	2mm 2.5mm	2.75mm 3mm 3.25mm	3.5mm 3.75mm 4mm	4.5mm	5mm 5.5mm	6mm 6.5mm 7mm 8mm	9mm 10mm
	Old UK	14 13	12 11 10	n/a 9 8	7	6 5	4 3 2 0	00 000
	US	0 1	2 n/a 3	4 5 6	7	8 9	10 10½ n/a 11	13 15
Yarn weight		Lace, 2-ply, fingering	Superfine, 3-ply, fingering, baby	Fine, 4-ply, sport, baby	Double knit (DK), light worsted, 5–6-ply	Aran, medium, worsted, Afghan, 12-ply	Bulky, chunky, craft, rug, 14-ply	Super bulky, super chunky, bulky, roving, 16-ply and upwards
What do you want to knit?		Lace	Fine-knit socks, shawls, babywear	Light sweaters, babywear, socks, accessories	Sweaters, light-weight scarves, blankets, toys	Sweaters, cables menswear, blankets, hats, scarves, mittens	Rugs, jackets, blankets, hats, leg warmers, winter accessories	Heavy blankets, rugs, thick scarves

Double knit (DK)/Light worsted/ 5–6-ply DK yarn is used for anything from blankets and toys to jumpers and cardigans. It is commonly associated with 4mm (UK8/US6) needles, and knits up quickly. Many projects in this book are knitted in DK yarn.

Aran/Worsted/12-ply A thick, warm yarn that requires 5mm (UK6/US8) needles. It is good for men's garments with thick cabled detail, and functional items. Many yarns in this thickness employ a variety of fibres to make them machine-washable.

Bulky/chunky/14-ply Although bulky, the yarn consists mainly of lightweight fibres to prevent garments from misshaping. Commonly worked on 7mm (UK2/USn/a) needles, it makes a chunky knitted fabric perfect for outerwear, hats, and leg warmers.

Super bulky/Super chunky/ 16-ply+ The yarn thickness varies, but it is mostly used with large needles from 10mm (UK000/US15) upwards. A great choice for beginners as stitches are so large that mistakes are easily visible. Good for rugged scarves.

Straight needles

If you are new to knitting, start with straight needles because they give a great deal of support to the hand when knitting. Short needles are recommended for small projects; longer needles are more suitable for wider knits such as a pullover or a baby's blanket, and for knitters who like to work by holding the needles underneath their arms or elbows.

Needles are sold in different sizes

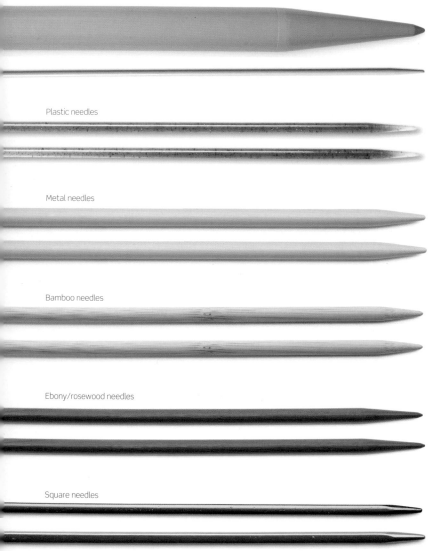

Plastic needles

Metal needles

Bamboo needles

Ebony/rosewood needles

Square needles

Size Knitting needles vary in diameter, from just 1.5mm (¹⁄₁₆in) thick to over 25mm (1in). There are three common needle-sizing systems: European metric, old British sizes, and American sizes. If you have older needles, use a knitting needle gauge to find their equivalent modern size. Needles are also available in various lengths to suit different projects and different ways of holding needles.

Plastic needles For needles with a surface that is halfway between that of metal and that of bamboo, choose plastic. It remains at a steady temperature during use, which may suit people who have arthritis. Avoid plastic needles of 4mm (UK8/US6) or smaller, as heavy projects may bend or break them.

Metal needles When working with hairy fibres such as mohair or wool, which may stick, slippery metal needles are great. If you find that you tend to knit too tightly, the slippery surface can help as it will cause a knitter's tension to loosen. Needles of more than 8mm (UK0/US11) in diameter can be clunky to work with, so are rarely available.

Bamboo needles Bamboo is a lightweight, flexible material, and makes excellent knitting needles. It helps to keep stitches regularly spaced, creating an even knitted fabric with a good tension. Great for slippery fibres such as silk and bamboo yarn. Recommended for arthritis sufferers. Thin needles will gradually warp slightly with use, to fit the curvature of your hand.

Ebony/rosewood needles These wooden needles feel luxurious to work with, and can be quite expensive. They often have a waxy surface, which becomes smooth with wear, creating a soft and tactile surface. Like bamboo needles, they help to create an even tension; they hold their shape and remain straight when used, giving them a solid feel.

Square needles Most needles are cylindrical with a pointed tip; these unusual new needles have a faceted surface and a pointed tip. Made from metal, they lie over each other better, which is particularly useful when working with double-pointed needles, and cause less strain on the hands, making them especially suitable for arthritis sufferers.

Other equipment

Hundreds of different gadgets are available to knitters. Some are merely for convenience, whereas others are absolutely vital and perform specific tasks. Here are the basics, to which you can add more advanced items as you progress. These basic items should always be at hand when you are working on a project. Most knitters have a portable knitting bag or case to keep them in, so that it is easy to take everything to wherever they want to sit and knit. The tools below are relatively inexpensive, and can be purchased from haberdashery stores and knitting suppliers.

Tape measure

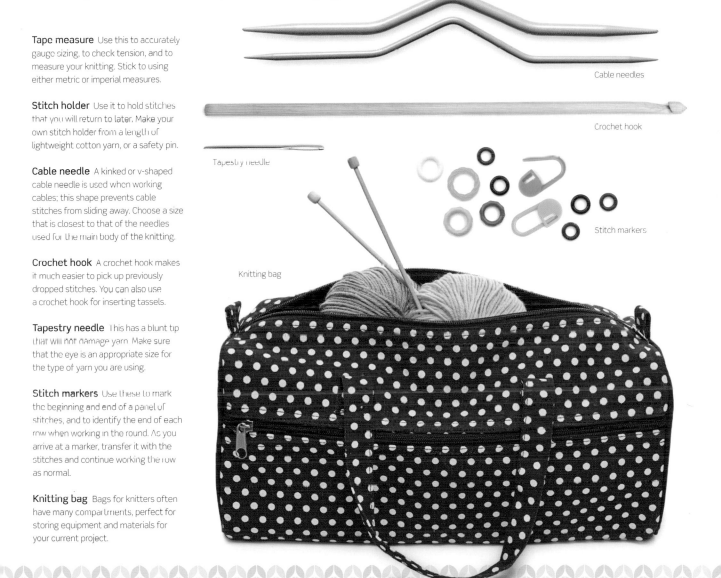

Stitch holder

Cable needles

Crochet hook

Tapestry needle

Stitch markers

Knitting bag

Tape measure Use this to accurately gauge sizing, to check tension, and to measure your knitting. Stick to using either metric or imperial measures.

Stitch holder Use it to hold stitches that you will return to later. Make your own stitch holder from a length of lightweight cotton yarn, or a safety pin.

Cable needle A kinked or v-shaped cable needle is used when working cables; this shape prevents cable stitches from sliding away. Choose a size that is closest to that of the needles used for the main body of the knitting.

Crochet hook A crochet hook makes it much easier to pick up previously dropped stitches. You can also use a crochet hook for inserting tassels.

Tapestry needle This has a blunt tip that will not damage yarn. Make sure that the eye is an appropriate size for the type of yarn you are using.

Stitch markers Use these to mark the beginning and end of a panel of stitches, and to identify the end of each row when working in the round. As you arrive at a marker, transfer it with the stitches and continue working the row as normal.

Knitting bag Bags for knitters often have many compartments, perfect for storing equipment and materials for your current project.

Following a pattern

Knitting patterns can look daunting to a beginner knitter, but if approached step by step they are easy to understand. This section provides an explanation of how to follow simple knitting patterns and gives tips for finishing details and seams. The best advice for a beginner wanting to knit a first project from a knitting pattern is to start with a simple accessory. Cushion covers are especially good practice as the instructions are straightforward and usually the only finishing details are seams. This is an example of a pattern for a simple, striped, stocking stitch cushion cover.

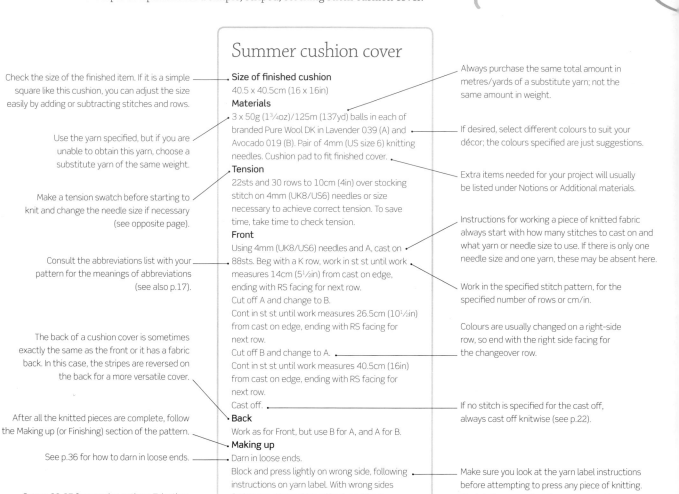

Summer cushion cover

Size of finished cushion
40.5 x 40.5cm (16 x 16in)

Materials
3 x 50g (1¾oz)/125m (137yd) balls in each of branded Pure Wool DK in Lavender 039 (A) and Avocado 019 (B). Pair of 4mm (US size 6) knitting needles. Cushion pad to fit finished cover.

Tension
22sts and 30 rows to 10cm (4in) over stocking stitch on 4mm (UK8/US6) needles or size necessary to achieve correct tension. To save time, take time to check tension.

Front
Using 4mm (UK8/US6) needles and A, cast on 88sts. Beg with a K row, work in st st until work measures 14cm (5½in) from cast on edge, ending with RS facing for next row.
Cut off A and change to B.
Cont in st st until work measures 26.5cm (10½in) from cast on edge, ending with RS facing for next row.
Cut off B and change to A.
Cont in st st until work measures 40.5cm (16in) from cast on edge, ending with RS facing for next row.
Cast off.

Back
Work as for Front, but use B for A, and A for B.

Making up
Darn in loose ends.
Block and press lightly on wrong side, following instructions on yarn label. With wrong sides facing, sew three sides of back and front together. Turn right-side out, insert cushion pad, and sew remaining seam.

Check the size of the finished item. If it is a simple square like this cushion, you can adjust the size easily by adding or subtracting stitches and rows.

Use the yarn specified, but if you are unable to obtain this yarn, choose a substitute yarn of the same weight.

Make a tension swatch before starting to knit and change the needle size if necessary (see opposite page).

Consult the abbreviations list with your pattern for the meanings of abbreviations (see also p.17).

The back of a cushion cover is sometimes exactly the same as the front or it has a fabric back. In this case, the stripes are reversed on the back for a more versatile cover.

After all the knitted pieces are complete, follow the Making up (or Finishing) section of the pattern.

See p.36 for how to darn in loose ends.

See pp.36-37 for seaming options. Take time with seams on knitting. Practise on odd pieces of knitting before starting your main project.

Always purchase the same total amount in metres/yards of a substitute yarn; not the same amount in weight.

If desired, select different colours to suit your décor; the colours specified are just suggestions.

Extra items needed for your project will usually be listed under Notions or Additional materials.

Instructions for working a piece of knitted fabric always start with how many stitches to cast on and what yarn or needle size to use. If there is only one needle size and one yarn, these may be absent here.

Work in the specified stitch pattern, for the specified number of rows or cm/in.

Colours are usually changed on a right-side row, so end with the right side facing for the changeover row.

If no stitch is specified for the cast off, always cast off knitwise (see p.22).

Make sure you look at the yarn label instructions before attempting to press any piece of knitting. The label may say that the yarn cannot be pressed or to press it only with a cool iron. (See p.36 for blocking tips.)

Garment patterns

Choosing the right size and knitting a tension swatch are the two most important things to get right if you want to create a successful garment. It is also possible to make simple alterations to patterns worked in plain garter or stocking stitch.

Choosing a garment size

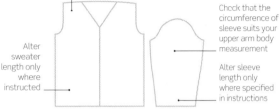

Choose your size by the width of a favourite, well-fitting sweater with the same shape and knitted fabric weight

Check that the circumference of sleeve suits your upper arm body measurement

Alter sweater length only where instructed

Alter sleeve length only where specified in instructions

Rather than looking at specific "sizes" when choosing which size to knit, select the one nearest to how you want the garment to fit. The best way to do this is to find a similar garment that fits you. Lay it flat and measure its width – choose the width on the pattern that is the closest match to your body shape.

Photocopy your pattern and highlight the figures for your size throughout. Start with the number of balls of yarn, then the number of stitches to cast on, the length to knit to the armhole, and so on. The smallest size is given first and larger sizes follow in parentheses. Where only one figure is given, this applies to all sizes.

Altering patterns

Alter the length of garment patterns worked in plain garter or stocking stitch, but avoid altering armholes, necklines, or sleeve heads. As sleeves and some bodies have shaping, this must also be adjusted. In this example, length is added to a sleeve:

1 Photocopy or draw out the pattern diagram. Write the new required length on the diagram (eg 48cm (19in)).

2 Find the number of rows to 10cm (4in) in the tension note. Divide number by 10 to calculate how many rows there are in 1cm. For example, 30 rows per 10cm (4in). 30 ÷ 10 = 3 rows per 1cm (½in).

3 Multiply the required new length by the number of rows in 1cm (½in). The resulting figure is the total number in the new length. For example, 48 × 3 = 144 rows.

4 Any increasing will also have to be re-calculated. From the pattern, note the number of stitches to cast on at the cuff and how many there will be on the needle just before the start of the underarm shaping (this figure should be shown at the end of the written instruction for the increases).

5 Subtract the smallest from the largest amount of stitches. The answer is the total number of stitches to be increased. Divide the answer by two (because a sleeve has two sides), to give the number of stitches to increase on each side. For example, 114 - 60 = 54 sts. 54 ÷ 2 = 27 sts.

6 To calculate the number of rows between each increase, divide the new number of rows found in Step 3 by the number of increases calculated in Step 5. If you have a fraction in this answer, round the number down. For example, 144 ÷ 27 = 4.22. Increase one stitch each side every 4 rows. Knit the remaining rows straight before underarm cast offs.

Measuring tension

Always knit a swatch before starting your project to make sure that you achieve the recommended stitch size (tension). Only if you achieve the correct tension will your knitting have the correct measurements.

1 Using the specified needle size, knit a 13cm (5in) square. Mark 10cm (4in) across the centre with pins and count the number of stitches between the pins.

2 Count the number of rows to 10cm (4in) in the same way. If you have fewer stitches and rows than you should, try again with a smaller needle size; if you have more, change to a larger needle. Use the needle size for your knitting that best matches the correct tension. (Matching stitch width is more important than matching row height.)

Understanding written instructions

Anyone who can cast on, knit and purl, and cast off will be able to work from simple knit-and-purl-combination stitch pattern instructions with little difficulty. It is just a question of following the instructions one step at a time and getting used to the abbreviations. A list of common knitting abbreviations is given opposite, but for simple knit and purl textures all you need to grasp is that "k1" means "knit one stitch", "k2" means "knit two stitches", and so on. And the same applies for the purl stitches – "p1" means "purl one stitch", "p2" means "purl two stitches", and so on.

To begin a stitch pattern, cast on the number of stitches that it tells you to, using your chosen yarn and the yarn manufacturer's recommended needle size. Work the stitch row by row, then repeat the rows as instructed and the stitch pattern will grow beneath the needles. When your knitting is the desired size, cast off in pattern (see pp.22-24).

The best tips for first-timers are to follow the rows slowly; mark the right side of the fabric by knotting a coloured thread onto it; use a row counter to keep track of where you are; and pull out your stitches and start again if you get in a muddle. If you love the stitch pattern you are trying out, you can make a scarf, blanket, or cushion cover with it – no need to buy a knitting pattern.

The principles for following stitch patterns are the same for lace and cables. Some stitch patterns will call for "slipping" stitches and knitting "through the back of the loop". To learn more about knitting terminlogy, consult the table (opposite) for the most common knitting abbreviations.

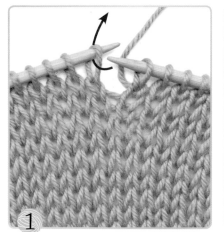

Slipping stitches purlwise

1 Always slip stitches purlwise, for example when slipping stitches onto a stitch holder, unless instructed otherwise. Insert the tip of the right needle from right to left through the front of the loop on the left needle.

2 Slide the stitch onto the tip of the right needle and off the left needle without working it. The slipped stitch now sits on the right needle with the right side of the loop at the front just like the worked stitches next to it.

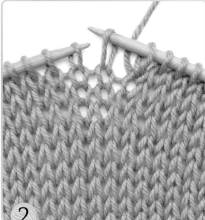

Slipping stitches knitwise

1 Slip stitches knitwise only if instructed to do so, or if working decreases (see pp.34-35), as it twists the stitch. First insert the tip of the right needle from left to right through the front of the loop on the left needle.

2 Slide the stitch onto the right needle and off the left needle without working it. The slipped stitch now sits on the right needle with the left side of the loop at the front of the needle unlike the worked stitches next to it.

Symbols, charts, and abbreviations

Knitting instructions for stitch patterns can also be given in chart form. Some knitters prefer working with stitch-symbol charts because they are easy to read, and they build up a visual image of the stitch repeat that is quick to memorize.

Even with charted instructions, there are usually written directions for how many stitches to cast on. If not, you can calculate the cast on from the chart, where the number of stitches in the pattern "repeat" are clearly marked. Cast on a multiple of this number, plus any edge stitches, three stitches are shown on the example chart, below, outside the six-stitch repeat.

Each square represents one knitted stitch and each horizontal line of squares represents a row on your knitted fabric. After casting on, work from the bottom of the chart upwards to start creating the knitted fabric. Read odd-numbered rows (usually RS rows) from right to left and even-numbered rows (usually WS rows) from left to right. Work the edge stitches, then work the stitches inside the repeat as many times as required. Some symbols may mean one thing on a RS row and another on a WS row (see below).

Once you have worked all the charted rows, start again at the bottom of the chart to begin the "row repeat" once more.

Charts

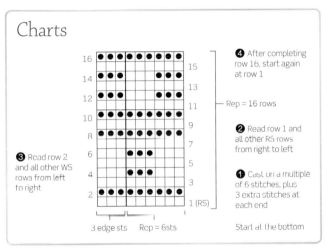

❹ After completing row 16, start again at row 1

Rep = 16 rows

❷ Read row 1 and all other RS rows from right to left

❸ Read row 2 and all other WS rows from left to right

❶ Cast on a multiple of 6 stitches, plus 3 extra stitches at each end

Start at the bottom

3 edge sts   Rep = 6sts

Knitting abbreviations

These are the most frequently used knitting abbreviations found both in this book and in popular knitting patterns throughout the world. Any special abbreviations in knitting instructions are always explained within the pattern.

alt alternate

beg begin(ning)

cm centimetre(s)

cont continu(e)(ing)

dec decrease(e)(ing)

foll follow(s)(ing)

g gram(s)

g st garter stitch

in inch(es)

inc increase(e)(ing)

k knit

k1 tbl knit st through back of loop

k2tog (or dec 1) knit next 2sts together (see p.34)

kfb (or inc 1) knit into front and back of next st

LH left hand

m metre(s)

M1 (or M1k) make one stitch (see pp.30–31)

mm millimetre(s)

oz ounce(s)

p purl

p2tog (or dec 1) purl next 2sts together (see p.34)

patt pattern, or work in pattern

Pfb (or inc 1) purl into front and back of next st (see p.29)

psso pass slipped stitch over

rem remain(s)(ing)

rep repeat(ing)

rev st st reverse stocking stitch

RH right hand

RS right side (of work)

s1 k1 psso (skpo) slip one, knit one, pass slipped st over (see p.35)

s1 k2tog psso (or sk2p) slip one st, knit 2sts together, pass slipped sts over

ssk slip, slip, knit (see p.35)

s slip stitch(es)

s2 k1 p2sso (or s2kpo) slip 2, knit one, pass slipped stitches over

st(s) stitch(es)

st st stocking stitch

tbl through back of loop(s)

tog together

WS wrong side (of work)

yd yard(s)

yfwd yarn forward (US yo; see p.32)

yfrn yarn forward round needle (US yo; see p.33)

yon yarn over needle (US yo; see p.33)

yrn yarn round needle (US yo; see p.32)

[ ] * Repeat the instructions between the brackets, or after or between the asterisks, as many times as instructed in the pattern

Stitch symbols

These are some of the commonly used knitting symbols in this book. Any unusual symbols will be explained in the pattern. Symbols can vary, so follow the explanations in your pattern.

☐	K on RS rows, p on WS rows
●	P on RS rows, k on WS rows
O	Yarnover
◿	K2tog
◺	Ssk
△	S1 k2tog psso (sk2p)
▵	Sk2 k1 p2sso (s2kpo)

Holding yarn and needles

Learning to knit is a very quick process. There are only a few initial techniques to pick up before you are ready to make simple shapes, such as scarves, blankets, and cushion covers. Basics include casting stitches onto the needles, knit and purl stitches, and casting stitches off the needles. Before starting to knit, familiarize yourself with how to hold the yarn and needles. See below for two common methods.

Knitting English style

1 Wrap yarn around fingers on your right hand. The aim is to control the yarn firmly but with a relaxed hand. Release the yarn to flow through fingers as the stitches are formed.

2 You need to be able to tension the yarn just enough with your fingers to create even stitches that are neither too loose nor too tight.

3 Hold the needles with the stitches about to be worked in the left hand and the working needle in the right hand. Use the right forefinger to wrap the yarn around the needle.

Knitting Continental style

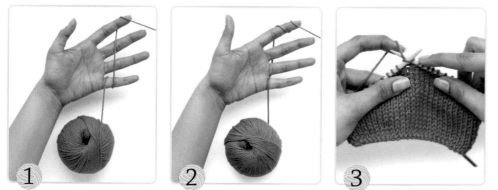

1 Wrap the yarn around the fingers of your left hand in any way that feels comfortable. Try this technique to see if you can both release and tension the yarn easily to create uniform loops.

2 This alternative tensioning technique may suit you better. Here the yarn is wrapped twice around the forefinger.

3 Hold the needle with the unworked stitches in the left hand and the working needle in the right. Position the yarn with the left forefinger and pull it through the loops with the right needle.

Making a slip knot

After reading about the two knitting styles on the previous page you are now ready to place the first loop of yarn on your needle and start creating a piece of knitting. This initial loop is called the slip knot and it is the first stitch formed when casting on stitches.

1 Begin by crossing the yarn coming from the ball over the yarn end (called the yarn tail) to form a large circle, or loop, of yarn.

2 Insert the tip of a knitting needle through the circle of yarn, then wrap the needle tip around the ball end of the yarn and pull the yarn through the circle.

3 This forms a loop on the needle and a loose, open knot below the loop.

4 Pull both ends of the yarn firmly to tighten the knot and the loop on the needle.

5 Make sure the completed slip knot is tight enough on the needle that it will not fall off but not so tight that you can barely slide it along the needle.

6 The yarn tail on the slip knot should be at least 10–15cm (4–6in) long so it can be threaded onto a blunt-ended yarn needle and darned in later. Your knitting pattern, however, may instruct you to leave an extra-long yarn tail (called a long loose end) to use for seams or other purposes.

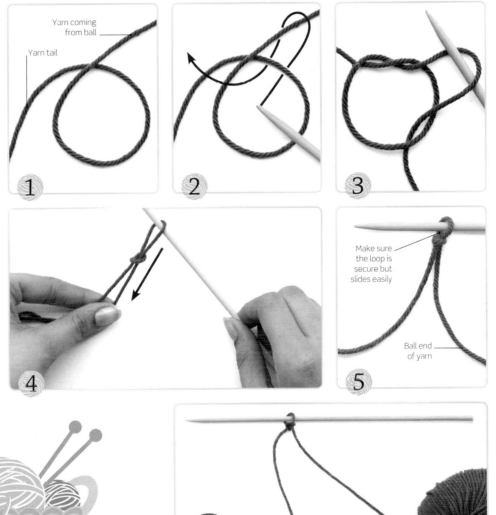

1. Yarn coming from ball — Yarn tail

5. Make sure the loop is secure but slides easily — Ball end of yarn

6. Extra-long yarn tail

Single strand cast ons

Casting on gives a closed edge to your knitting that won't unravel. There are several methods of casting on, but the basic techniques shown here are the quickest and simplest ways to get started.

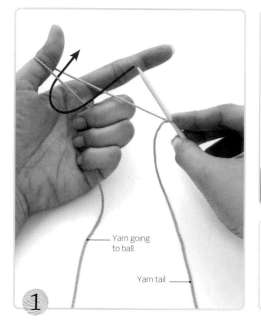

Yarn going to ball

Yarn tail

1

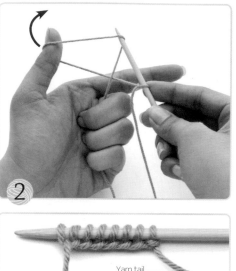

2

Yarn tail

Yarn going to ball

3

Single cast on
(also called thumb cast on)

1 This is the easiest cast on technique. Hold the needle with the slip knot in your right hand. Then wrap the yarn around your left thumb as shown and hold the yarn in place in the palm of your left hand. Insert the needle tip under and up through the loop on your thumb following the arrow.

2 Release the loop from your thumb and pull the yarn to tighten the new cast on loop on the needle, sliding it up close to the slip knot.

3 Loop the yarn around your thumb again and continue making loops in the same way until the required number of stitches is on the needle.

Knit on cast on
(also called knit stitch cast on)

1 Place the needle with the slip knot in your left hand. Insert tip of right needle from left to right through centre of loop on left needle. With yarn behind needles, wrap it under and around tip of right needle. (While casting on, use your left forefinger to hold loops on left needle in position.) Using tip of right needle, carefully draw yarn through loop on left needle.

2 Transfer the loop on the right needle to the left needle by inserting the left needle from right to left through the front of the loop. Pull both yarn ends to tighten the new cast on loop on the needle, sliding it up close to the slip knot.

3 Continue casting on stitches in the same way for the required number of stitches. For a looser cast on, hold two needles together in your left hand while casting on.

Yarn going to ball

2

Long yarn tail

1

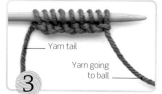

Yarn tail

Yarn going to ball

3

Yarn going to ball

Long yarn tail

1

2

3

Cable cast on

1 Begin by working Steps 1–2 of the knit on cast on (opposite). Then insert the tip of the right needle between the two loops on the left needle and wrap the yarn under and around the tip of the right needle.

2 With the tip of the right needle, draw the yarn through to form a loop on the right needle.

3 Transfer the loop on the right needle to the left needle (see Step 2 Knit on cast on). Continue, inserting the needle between the first two loops on the left needle when beginning each new cast on stitch.

Finger loop cast on

1 This gives a soft cast on. Hold the needle with the slip knot in your right hand. Lift the yarn from underneath with your left index finger pointing away from you. Bend and turn your finger to point towards you.

2 Insert the needle into the loop that lies on top of your finger from behind.

3 Release your index finger and tighten the stitch on the needle.

1   **2**   **3**

TOP TIP *If your casting on is always too tight, use a needle one size larger*

Simple cast offs

When your piece of knitted fabric is complete you need to close off the loops so that they cannot unravel. This is called casting off the stitches. Although casting off is shown here worked across knit stitches, the principle is the same for purl stitches. If instructed to retain stitches for future use, slip your stitches onto a spare needle or a stitch holder.

Casting off knitwise

1 Begin by knitting the first two stitches. Then insert the tip of the left needle from left to right through the first stitch and lift this stitch up and over the second stitch and off the right needle.

2 To cast off the next stitch, knit one more stitch and repeat Step 1. Continue until only one stitch remains on the right needle. If your pattern says "cast off in pattern", work the stitches in the specified pattern as you cast off.

3 To stop the last stitch from unravelling, cut the yarn, leaving a yarn tail 20cm (8in) long, which is long enough to darn into the knitting later. (Alternatively, leave a much longer yarn end to use for a future seam.) Pass the yarn end through the remaining loop and pull tight to close the loop. This is called fastening off.

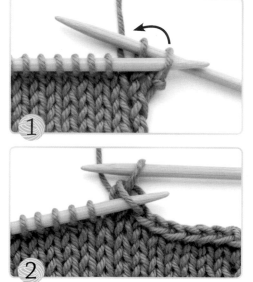

Slipping stitches off needle

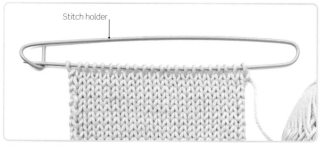

Stitch holder

Using a stitch holder: If you are setting stitches aside to work on later, your instructions will tell you whether to cut the yarn or keep it attached to the ball. Carefully slip your stitches onto a stitch holder large enough to hold all the stitches. If you are only slipping a few stitches, use a safety pin.

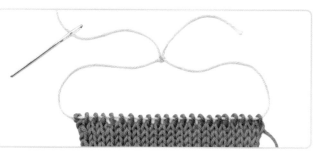

Using a length of yarn: If you do not have a stitch holder or do not have one large enough, use a length of cotton yarn instead. Using a blunt-ended yarn needle, pass the yarn through the stitches as you slip them off the knitting needle. Knot the ends of the cotton yarn together.

Alternative cast offs

Try using one of these casting off techniques to complement your project. Consider using a contrast colour, either in the basic cast off or combined with a decorative style. Cast offs are included that give more stretch to ribs or loosen an edge, and an adaptation of the three needle cast off can be used to join pockets and hems.

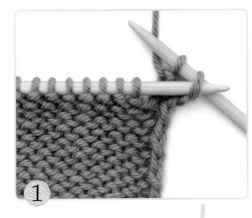

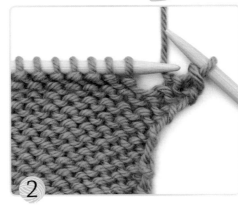

Purl cast off

1 Purl two stitches, then take the yarn to the back. Insert the tip of the left needle into the first stitch and pass it over the second stitch and off the right needle.

2 Bring the yarn to the front, repeat Steps 1 and 2 across row, but purl only one stitch in Step 1. Pull the end stitch through itself as for casting off knitwise (see opposite).

Casting off in rib effect

Use after a single rib fabric to maintain the rib corrugations. This method adds a little more stretch than casting off in either all knit or all purl.

1 Work one knit and one purl. Move the yarn to the back. Insert the left needle into the first stitch. Pass over the second and off the right needle.

2 Knit the next stitch then pass the first stitch over the second and off the right needle as before.

3 Yarn to front and purl next stitch. Repeat Steps 2 and 3 across the row. Pull the final stitch through itself to fasten off.

Tubular cast off

1 In preparation, and over an even number of stitches, work two rows as follows: knit the first stitch, bring yarn to front and slip the purl stitch that follows without twisting it (purlwise), take yarn to back. Repeat across row.

2 Stretch your ribbing out and cut the yarn end to about four times the length of the required cast off edge. Thread onto a blunt-ended yarn needle. Hold the knitting with the tip to the right. Insert the yarn needle into the first stitch knitwise. Pull the yarn through and drop the stitch.

3 Bring the yarn across the front and insert the needle purlwise into the third (knit) stitch. Pull the yarn through but not too tightly. Take it to the right and insert purlwise into the second (purl) stitch, taking the yarn through to the back.

4 Take the yarn behind the third (knit) stitch, bring it to the front between the third and fourth stitch and insert it as shown into the fourth (purl) stitch. Then insert the needle through the centre of the preceding knit stitch, and out to the front around the left leg.

5 Repeat Steps 3–4. Tension the stitches evenly as you work.

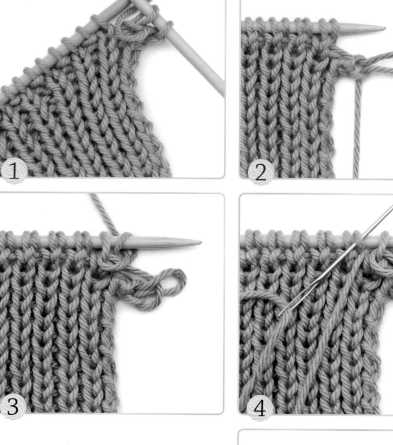

TOP TIP   *Thread the yarn gently for a straight edge.*

Knit and purl stitches

All knitting is made up of only two basic stitches – knit and purl. These examples are shown on stocking stitch. The purl stitch is a little more difficult, but becomes effortless with practise. Once you are a seasoned knitter, your hands will know how to work these basic stitches in your sleep. Work your first purl row after you have cast on and knitted a few rows of garter stitch (see p.26).

Knit stitch (abbreviation: k)

1 Hold needle with unworked stitches in your left hand and other needle in your right hand. With yarn at back of knitting, insert right needle from left to right under front loop and through centre of next stitch to be worked on left needle.

2 Wrap yarn under and around right needle, keeping an even tension as the yarn slips through your fingers.

3 With right needle, draw yarn through stitch on left needle. Hold yarn reasonably firmly. Let old loop drop off left needle to complete knit stitch on right needle. Work all stitches on left needle onto right needle in same way. To start new row, turn work and transfer right needle to left hand.

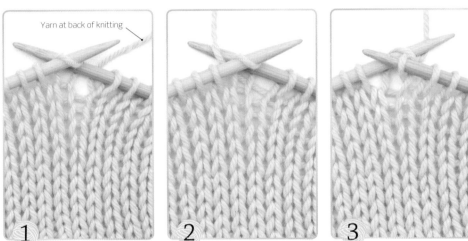

Yarn at back of knitting

Purl stitch (abbreviation: p)

1 With yarn at front of knitting, insert right needle from right to left through centre of next stitch to be worked on left needle. Wrap yarn over and around right needle. Keep an even tension on yarn as you release it.

2 With needle, draw yarn through stitch on left needle. Keep your hands relaxed and allow yarn to slip through fingers in a controlled manner.

3 Let old loop drop off left needle to complete purl stitch. Work all stitches on left needle onto right needle in the same way. To start next row, turn work and transfer the knitting to your left hand.

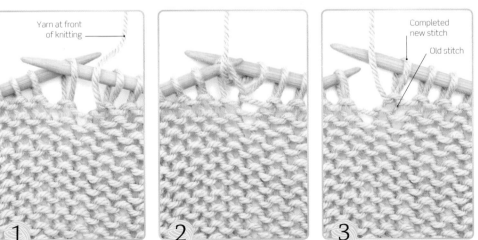

Yarn at front of knitting

Completed new stitch

Old stitch

Basic pattern stitches

Once you know how to work knit and purl stitch with ease, you will be able to work the most frequently used stitch patterns – garter stitch and stocking stitch. Stocking stitch and reverse stocking stitch are commonly used for plain knitted garments and many more complicated patterns are based on these stitches.

Garter stitch (abbreviation: g st)

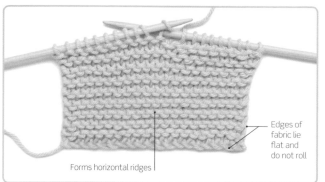

Forms horizontal ridges

Edges of fabric lie flat and do not roll

Knit right side (RS) rows: Garter stitch is the easiest of all knitted fabrics because whichever side is facing you, all rows are worked in knit stitch. When the right side of the fabric is facing you, knit all the stitches in the row. Both sides look the same. The resulting fabric is soft, textured, and slightly stretchy. More rows are needed than in stocking stitch to make the same length of fabric.

Single ribbing (abbreviation: k1, p1 rib)

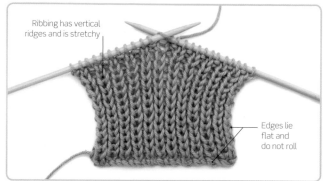

Ribbing has vertical ridges and is stretchy

Edges lie flat and do not roll

Right side (RS) rows: Single ribbing is formed by working alternating knit and purl stitches over an even number of stitches. Bring the yarn forwards before working the second (purl) stitch, and take it backwards before the third (knit) stitch, and so on. Both sides look the same and are worked in the same way. Ribbed fabric is stretchy and, therefore, ideal for cuffs and collars on knitted sweaters.

Stocking stitch (abbreviation: st st)

Side edges roll slightly to back

Right side is smooth

Bottom edge naturally rolls up at front

Knit right side (RS) rows: Stocking stitch is formed by working alternate rows of knit and purl stitches. When the right side is facing you, knit all the stitches in the row.

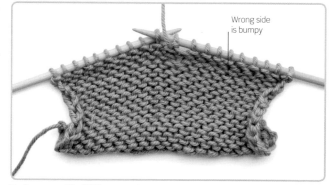

Wrong side is bumpy

Purl wrong side (WS) rows: When the wrong side is facing you, purl all the stitches in the row. The wrong side is often referred to as the "purl side".

Joining yarn

To calculate if there is sufficient yarn to complete two rows, fold the remaining yarn in half and make a slip knot at the fold. Knit the first row. If the knot comes before the end of the row you do not have enough yarn and need to join on a fresh ball.

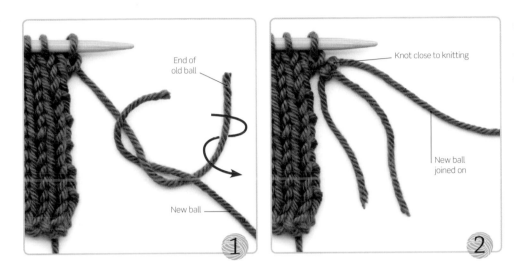

End of old ball

New ball

Knot close to knitting

New ball joined on

Joining on a new ball

1 Always join on a new ball at the beginning of a row. Knot the new end of yarn onto the old yarn.

2 Slide the knot up very close to the edge of the knitting. The knot can be hidden in the seam later. If you are knitting a scarf or blanket, tie the knot loosely so you can undo it later and darn in the ends.

Weaver's knot

Use this knot when joining yarns of different thickness.

1 Make a loop of the thick yarn and pinch the neck together. Thread a longish end of the thin yarn through the loop from above, and wrap it over the neck of the loop from back to front, pinch this to the loop with your fingers.

2 Take the thin yarn end that is wrapped around the loop under the front thread of the thick yarn loop. Pass it over itself as you take it towards the back and then pass it under the rear thread of the thick yarn loop.

3 Holding both thick yarns in one hand and both thin in the other, gently pull the short ends apart with your fingers to close the knot.

Square knot

This is made like a granny knot, but take left over right, then right over left. This is best made at the point where it is needed in the knitting so you can make sure it goes to the back.

Correcting mistakes

The best thing to do if you make a mistake in your knitting is to unravel it back to the mistake by unpicking the stitches one by one. If you drop a stitch, be sure to pick it up quickly before it comes undone right back to the cast on edge.

Unpicking a knit row

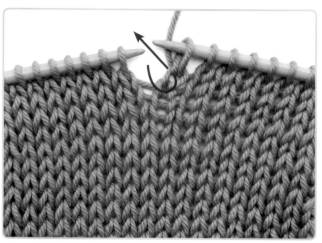

Unravelling on RS: Hold the needle with the stitches in your right hand. To unpick each stitch individually, insert the tip of the left needle from front to back through the stitch below the first knit stitch on the right needle, then drop the old knit stitch off the needle and pull out the loop.

Unpicking a purl row

Unravelling on WS: Hold the needle with the stitches in your right hand. Unpick each purl stitch individually with the tip of the left needle in the same way as for the knit stitch. When unpicking stitches, do not split the yarn or you will add two stitches to your needle. Count the stitches before you start knitting again.

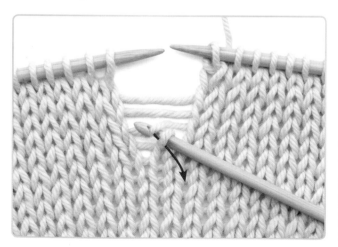

Picking up a dropped stitch

Reclaim a dropped stitch on st st: You can easily reclaim a dropped stitch with a crochet hook. With the right side of the knitting facing you, insert the hook through the dropped loop. Grab the strand between the stitches and pull a loop through the loop on the hook. Continue up the rows in this way until you reach the top. Then slip the stitch back onto your needle.

Simple increases

Increasing the number of stitches on the needle is one way knitting is shaped, changing the edges from straight vertical sides to curves and slants. The following techniques are simple increases used for shaping knitting.

Knit into front and back of stitch

(abbreviation: kfb or inc 1)

This popular invisible increase for a knit row is also called a bar increase because it creates a little bar between the stitches.

1 Knit the next stitch, leaving the stitch being worked on the left needle. Insert the right needle through the back of the loop from right to left.

2 Wrap the yarn around the tip of the right needle, draw the yarn through the loop to form the second stitch and drop the old stitch off the left needle.

3 Knitting into both the front and the back of the stitch creates two new stitches out of one, and increases one stitch overall in the row.

New stitch

Purl into front and back of stitch (abbreviation: pfb or inc 1)

New stitch

1 Purl the next stitch, leaving the stitch being worked on the left needle. Insert the right needle through the back of the loop from left to right.

2 Wrap the yarn around the tip of the right needle, draw the yarn through the loop to form the second stitch and drop the old stitch off the left needle.

3 Purling into the front and the back of the stitch like this creates two stitches out of one and increases one stitch in the row.

Lifted increase on knit row (abbreviation: inc 1)

1 Insert the tip of the right needle from front to back through the stitch below the next stitch on the left needle. Knit this lifted loop.

2 Knit the next stitch (the stitch above the lifted stitch on the left needle) in the usual way.

3 This creates two stitches out of one and increases one stitch in the row. (The purl version of this stitch is worked using the same principle.)

"Make one" left cross increase on a knit row (abbreviation: M1 or M1k)

1 Insert the tip of the left needle from front to back under the horizontal strand between the stitch just knit and the next stitch. Then insert the right needle through the strand on the left needle from right to left behind the left needle.

2 Wrap the yarn around the tip of the right needle and draw the yarn through the lifted loop. (This is called knitting through the back of the loop.)

3 This creates an extra stitch in the row. (Knitting through the back of the loop twists the base of the new stitch to produce a crossed stitch that closes up the hole it would have created.)

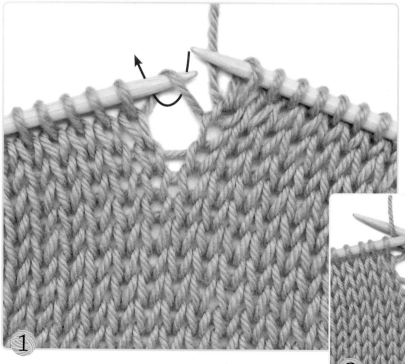

"Make one" right cross increase on a knit row (abbreviation: M1 or M1k)

Knitting patterns do not always differentiate between left and right "make one" increases. Choose the most suitable increase for your project.

1 Insert the tip of the left needle from back to front under the horizontal strand between the knitted stitch and the next one. Insert the right needle from left to right into the front of this new loop, twisting the stitch.

2 Wrap the yarn around the tip of the needle and draw the yarn through the lifted loop, knitting into the front of the stitch.

3 This action crosses the lifted stitch, and closes the hole made by picking up the loop. The resulting increase slants to the right and is normally worked at the end of a knit row.

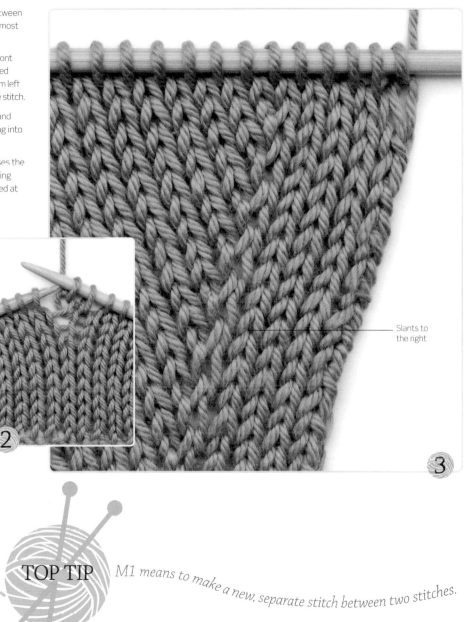

Slants to the right

TOP TIP *M1 means to make a new, separate stitch between two stitches.*

Yarnover increases

Also known as "visible increases", yarnover increases add stitches to a row and create holes at the same time. They are used to produce decorative lace patterns. A yarnover is made by looping the yarn around the right needle to form an extra stitch. It is important to wrap the loop around the needle in the correct way or it will become crossed when it is worked in the next row, which closes the hole.

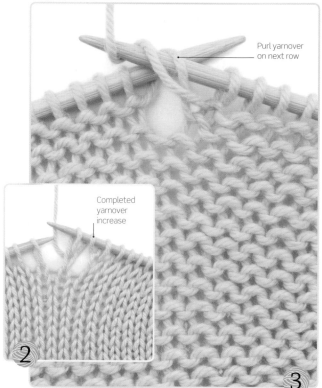

Purl yarnover on next row

Yarnover between knit stitches
(abbreviation: UK yfwd; US yo)

1 Bring the yarn forwards (yfwd) to the front of the knitting between the needles. Take the yarn over the top of the right needle to the back and work the next knit stitch in the usual way.

2 When the knit stitch is complete, the yarnover is correctly formed on the right needle with the right leg of the loop at the front.

3 On the following row, when you reach the yarnover, purl it through the front of the loop. This will create an open hole under the purl stitch.

Completed yarnover increase

Yarnover between purl stitches (abbreviation: UK yrn; US yo)

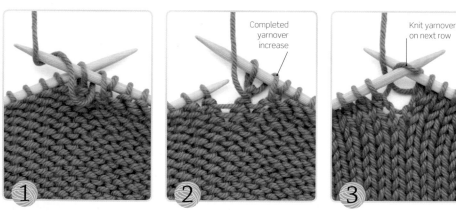

Completed yarnover increase

Knit yarnover on next row

1 Bring the yarn to the back of the work over the top of the right needle, then to the front between the needles. Work the next purl stitch in the usual way.

2 When the purl stitch is complete, the yarnover is correctly formed on the right needle with the right leg of the loop at the front of the needle.

3 On the following row, when you reach the yarnover, knit it through the front of the loop in the usual way. This creates an open hole under the knit stitch.

Yarnover between knit and purl stitches (abbreviation: UK yfrn and yon; US yo)

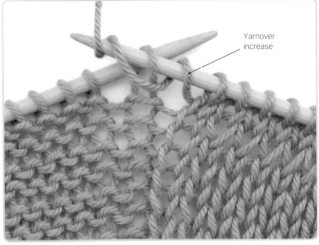

Yarnover increase

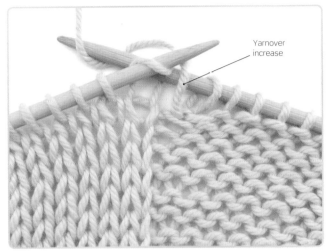

Yarnover increase

After a knit stitch and before a purl stitch (yfrn): Bring the yarn to the front between the needles, then over the top of the right needle and to the front again. Purl the next stitch. On the following row, work the yarnover through the front of the loop in the usual way to create an open hole.

After a purl stitch and before a knit stitch (yon): Take the yarn over the top of the right needle and to the back of the work, then knit the next stitch. On the following row, work the yarnover through the front of the loop in the usual way to create an open hole.

Yarnover at the beginning of a row (abbreviation: UK yfwd and yrn; US yo)

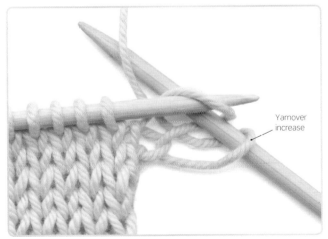

Yarnover increase

Yarnover increase

At the beginning of a row before a knit stitch (yfwd): Insert the right needle behind the yarn and into the first stitch knitwise. Take the yarn over the top of the right needle to the back and complete the knit stitch. On the following row, work yarnover through front of loop to create an open scallop at the edge.

At the beginning of a row before a purl stitch (yrn): Wrap the yarn from front to back over the top of the right needle and to the front again between the needles. Then purl the first stitch. On the following row, work the yarnover through the front of the loop in the usual way to create an open scallop at the edge.

Simple decreases

To shape knitting, and for creating textured stitches, when paired with increases, decreases are essential. Complicated decreases are always explained in knitting instructions. Most of the decreases that follow are single decreases that subtract only one stitch from the knitting, but the most common double decreases are included.

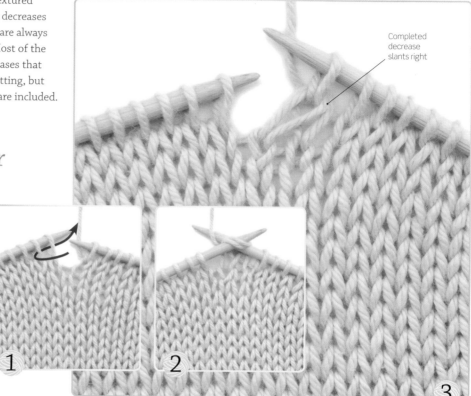

Completed decrease slants right

Knit two together

(abbreviation: k2tog or dec 1)

1 Insert the tip of the right needle from left to right through the second stitch then the first stitch on the left needle.

2 Wrap the yarn around the tip of the right needle, draw the yarn through both loops and drop the old stitches off the left needle.

3 This makes two stitches into one and decreases one stitch in the row. The completed stitch slants to the right.

Purl two together (abbreviation: p2tog or dec 1)

Completed decrease slants right

1 Use the p2tog decrease where a pattern specifies "decrease 1" on a purl row. Insert the tip of the right needle from right to left through the first, then the second stitch on the left needle.

2 Wrap the yarn around the tip of the right needle, draw the yarn through both loops and drop the old stitches off the left needle.

3 This makes two stitches into one and decreases one stitch in the row.

Slip one, knit one, pass slipped stitch over (abbeviation: s1 k1 psso or skpo)

1 Slip the first stitch on the left needle knitwise onto the right needle without working it. Then knit the next stitch.

2 Pick up the slipped stitch with the tip of the left needle and pass it over the knit stitch and off the right needle.

3 This makes two stitches into one and decreases one stitch in the row.

Slipped knitwise onto right needle

Completed decrease slants left

Slip, slip, knit

(abbreviation: ssk)

1 Slip the next two stitches on the left needle knitwise, one at a time, onto the tip of the right needle without working them.

2 Insert the tip of the left needle from left to right through the fronts of the two slipped stitches (the right needle is now behind the left). Knit these two stitches together.

3 This makes two stitches into one and decreases one stitch in the row.

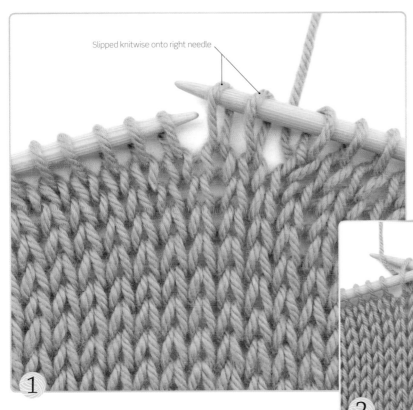

Slipped knitwise onto right needle

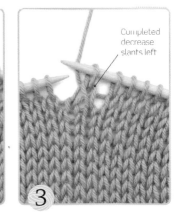

Completed decrease slants left

Seams and blocking

After you have finished knitting, and before you sew it together, your project will need blocking. This means to pin out and set the knitted shape using steam, or by wet-pressing. Always refer to the yarn label, or pattern instructions beforehand. Textured stitches may lose their shape when steam blocked.

Wet blocking

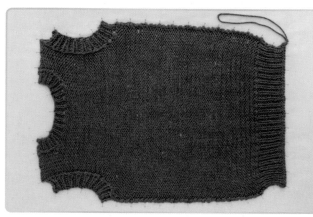

Wet the knitting: Wet blocking is the best way to even out your knitting on certain yarns (see ballband). Using lukewarm water, either wash the piece or simply wet it. Squeeze and lay it flat on a towel, then roll the towel to squeeze out more moisture. Pin the piece into shape on layers of dry towels covered with a sheet. Leave to dry.

Steam blocking

Steam the knitting: Only steam block if your yarn allows. Pin the piece to the correct shape, then place a clean damp cloth on top. Use a warm iron to create steam, barely touching the cloth. Do not rest the iron on the knitting, and avoid any garter stitch or ribbed areas. Before removing the pins, let the piece dry completely.

Darning in an end

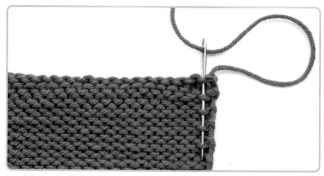

A professional finish: Completed knitting will have at least two yarn ends - one at the cast on and one at the cast off edges. For every extra ball used, there will be two more ends. Thread each end separately onto a large-eyed needle and weave it vertically or horizontally through stitches on the wrong side of your work.

Edge-to-edge seam

Suitable for most stitch patterns: Align the pieces of knitting with the wrong sides facing upwards. Using a large-eyed needle and matching yarn, sew the seam together through the little pips formed along the edges of knitting, as shown. Do not pull the seam too tight.

Backstitch seam

Right sides of
knitting together

Suitable for almost any seam on knitting: Align the pieces of knitting with the right sides together. Make one stitch forwards, and one stitch back into the starting point of the previous stitch as shown. Work the stitches as close to the edge of the knitting as possible. A backstitch seam is not suitable for super-bulky yarns.

Overcast seam

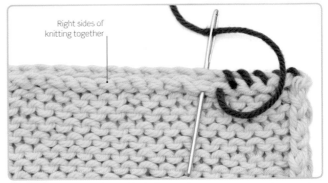

Right sides of
knitting together

Oversewn seam (or whipped stitch seam): With the right sides facing each other, insert the needle from back to front through both layers of knitted fabric, working through the centres of the edge stitches and not through the pips at the edge of the fabric. Create each stitch in the same way as you sew the seam together.

Grafted seam

This seam is worked along two pieces of knitting that have not been cast off or along two cast off edges as shown here; the principle for both is the same.

1 With the right sides facing you, follow the path of a row of knitting along the seam as shown. Do not pull the stitches too tight

2 When worked in a matching yarn as here, the seam blends in completely and makes it look like a continuous piece of knitting.

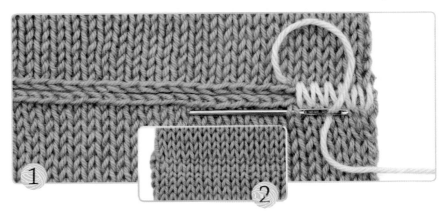

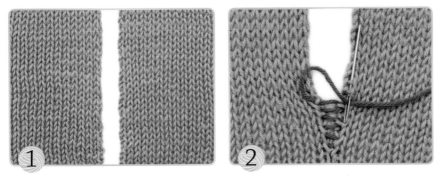

Mattress stitch

1 The best seam technique for ribbing and stocking stitch, mattress stitch is practically invisible. Start by aligning the edges of the pieces to be seamed with both right sides facing.

2 Insert the needle from front through centre of the first knit stitch on one piece of knitting and up through centre of stitch two rows above. Repeat on other piece, working up seam and pulling edges together every few stitches.

Rosette snood

This ladies' winter knit is worked in a medium-weight yarn spun from the fleece of Peruvian alpacas and sheep, making it both luxurious and thick, but any aran yarn will work just as well. The simple pattern is embellished with knitted rosettes.

Essential information

SIZE 36cm x 1.4m (14¼ x 55in)

YARN

Artesano Alpaca Aran/Berroco Ultra Alpaca 100g

A **B**

A: 2200 Laxford x 2/6258 Cyclamen x 2

B: 5003 Lomond x 1/6233 Rose Spice x 1

NEEDLES

A: 1 pair of 10mm (UK000/US15) needles
B: 1 pair of 7.5mm (UK1/USn/a) needles

A
B

TENSION

10sts and 12 rows to 10cm (4in) over patt on 10mm (UK000/US15) needles

NOTIONS

Large-eyed needle
3 x 2cm (¾in) mother-of-pearl buttons

Using needles A and yarn A, cast on 40sts.
ROW 1: K.
ROW 2: K.
ROW 3: *K1, p1, rep from * to end of row.
ROW 4: *K1, p1, rep from * to end of row.
Rep rows 1–4 until work measures 1.4m (55in).
Cast off loosely.
Sew cast on edge to cast off edge.
Block (see p.36).

Rosettes

Using needles B and yarn B, cast on 15sts.
ROW 1: K.
ROW 2: Kfb into every st.
ROW 3: K.
ROW 4: K.
ROW 5: Kfb into every st.
ROW 6: K.
ROW 7: K.
Cast off loosely.
Roll strip into flower shape, stitching as you go.
Attach button to centre of flower and sew flowers to snood.

Knitted rosettes An easy mini project, these pink roses "grow" when you knit into the front and back of each stitch to increase the fabric. They are attached to the snood with mother-of-pearl buttons.

TOP TIP *Add mother-of-pearl buttons for a delicate, shimmering finish.*

Striped snake scarf

This child's scarf, worked in moss stitch, is a simple project for a beginner. The cotton yarn is a joy to work with and the pattern is quick to complete. Finish your creation with a pom-pom tail.

Essential information

SIZE 15cm x 1.5m (6 x 59in)

YARN

Debbie Bliss DK Cotton 50g

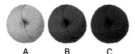

A   **B**   **C**

A: 20 Green x 2   **B:** 62 Blue x 2   **C:** 47 Red x 1

NEEDLES

1 pair of 4mm (UK8/US6) needles

TENSION

20sts by 30 rows to 10cm (4in) over st st on 4mm (UK8/US6) needles

NOTIONS

Large-eyed needle

SPECIAL ABBREVIATIONS

MB Make a bobble

Striped pattern

Using yarn A, k 10 rows.
Using yarn B, k 6 rows.
Rep throughout, until row 188, then cont in yarn B only.

Body

In yarn A cast on 2sts.
ROW 1: *K1, p1.
ROW 2: P1, k1.
Rep from *.
Cont in moss st as above and inc (kfb or pfb) into the first and last st every 4th row. Cont stripe as stated until you are left with 36sts and have 68 rows.
Cont knitting straight in moss st and foll the stripe layout until 177 rows have been knitted.
ROWS 178–188: Cont in moss st, dec 1st (k2tog or p2tog) at beg and end of row 178, row 182, and row 188. (30sts)
ROWS 189–200: Cont in moss st for 12 rows inc into first and last stitch every 2 rows. (42sts)
ROWS 201–225: Cont in moss st straight.
ROW 226: Cont in moss st. Dec 1st at beg and end of each row. At sts 17 and 23 MB, (using yarn A, k into front, back, front, back of st, turn, p4, turn, k4, turn, p4, k2, k2tog, then pass third and fourth sts over first st).
ROWS 227–242: Cont in moss st. Dec 1st at beginning and end of each row.
ROW 243: Change to yarn C. (8sts)
Cont knitting in moss st for 15 rows.

Forked tongue

ROW 259: *K1, p1, k1, p1, turn.
ROW 260: P1, k1, p1, k1, turn.
ROW 261: K1, p1, k1, p1, turn.
ROW 262: P1, k1, p1, k1, turn.
ROW 263: K1, p1, k1, p1, turn.
Break yarn and cast off these 4sts.
Reattach yarn to rem 4sts and rep from *.
Cast off.

Pom-pom

Cut two circles of card (6cm (2¹/₂in) diameter); cut a smaller circle out of the centre. Place two circles on top of each other. Wrap yarn C around the circle until there is no hole left in the centre (it is easier to wrap with small bundles of yarn). Using scissors, cut all the way around the edge of the circle, take a separate piece of yarn and wrap it around the middle of the pom-pom, making sure to go between the two pieces of circular card; secure tightly. Remove the card circles and puff up the pom-pom. Sew the pom-pom onto the bottom of the snake as a tail.

Floral ear warmer

This classic ribbed band is tapered at the back and embellished with a stylized flower worked as one piece in garter stitch. Knit this pattern in a cotton yarn for a lightweight headband that can be worn in warm weather.

Essential information

SIZE To fit an adult female

YARN

King Cole Baby Alpaca DK/Classic Elite Inca Alpaca 50g

A   **B**

A: 513 Lilac x 1/1179 Santo grape x 1
B: 501 Fawn x 1/1116 Natural x 1

NEEDLES

A: 1 pair of 3.25mm (UK10/US3) needles
B: 1 pair of 3mm (UK11/USn/a) needles

_____ A
_____ B

NOTIONS

1 x 2.5cm (1½in) button
Large-eyed needle

TENSION

35sts and 30 rows to 10cm (4in) over rib patt on 3.25mm (UK10/US3) needles

SPECIAL ABBREVIATIONS

M1K or **M1P** Make a stitch by picking up bar between sts and knitting or purling into back of it (see pp.28–29)

Headband

With needles A and yarn A, cast on 19sts.
ROW 1 (RS): K1, [p1, k1] to end.
ROW 2: P1, [k1, p1] to end.
These 2 rows form the rib.
Rib 2 rows more.

Shape sides

ROW 1: K1, M1k, rib to last st, M1k, k1.
ROW 2: P2, rib to last 2sts, p2.
ROW 3: K2, rib to last 2sts, k2.
ROW 4: As row 2.
ROW 5: K1, M1p, rib to last st, M1p, k1.
ROWS 6–8: Rib 3 rows straight.
Rep last 8 rows x 2, then work rows 1–5. (35sts)
Cont straight until work measures 40cm (16in) from beg, ending after WS row.

Shape sides

ROW 1: Skpo, rib to last 2sts, k2tog.
ROW 2: P2, rib to last 2sts, p2.
ROW 3: K2, rib to last 2sts, k2.
ROW 4: As row 2.
ROW 5: As row 1.
ROWS 6–8: Rib 3 rows straight.
Rep these 8 rows x 3. (19sts)
Cast off in rib.

Flower

Beg at centre. Using needles B and yarn B, cast on 5sts. K 1 row.
INC ROW: [Kfb] to end.
NEXT ROW: K.
Rep last 2 rows once more. (20sts)
NEXT ROW: [Kfb, k1] to end. (30sts)
K 1 row.

Divide for petals.
***NEXT ROW:** K6, turn.
K 4 rows on these 6sts.
NEXT 2 ROWS: K2, k2tog, k2; turn and k5.
NEXT 2 ROWS: K1, k2tog, k2; turn and k4.
NEXT ROW: [K2tog] x 2, then pass second st over first st and fasten off.**
Return to sts on LH needle.*
Rep from * to * x 3, then work from * to **.

Making up

Join first to last petal and neaten edges of flower. Join headband into a ring and sew cast on and cast off edges together. Sew flower in place, then sew button to centre of flower.

Tapered headband Shape the back of this easy-to-knit headband using the M1 increase, and the k2tog and skpo decrease techniques. Cast off in rib effect and sew a flat edge-to-edge seam to form the band.

Leg warmers

Worked in knit one, purl one rib, instructions are given here for both seamless leg warmers knitted in the round on four double-pointed needles, and for ones that can be knitted on two regular needles and seamed afterwards. The choice is yours.

Essential information

SIZE One size fits all, 55cm (22in) long

YARN

King Cole Merino Blend/Knit Picks Swish DK 50g

791 Denim x 4/Twilight x 4

NEEDLES

A: 4 x 3.75mm (UK9/US5) double-pointed needles, or 1 pair of 3.75mm (UK9/US5) needles

B: 4 x 4mm (UK8/US6) double-pointed needles, or 1 pair of 4mm (UK8/US6) needles

————————————————— A
————————————————— B

TENSION

22sts and 30 rows to 10cm (4in) over st st on 4mm (UK8/US6) needles

NOTIONS

Large-eyed needle

In the round (make 2)

With double-pointed needles A, cast on 60sts and distribute them evenly on 3 needles.
Work in rounds of k1, p1 rib for 5cm (2$^1/_4$in). Change to double-pointed needles B and cont in rib until your work measures 50cm (20in) from beg. Change to needles A and rib a further 5cm (2$^1/_4$in). Cast off in rib.

With seam (make 2)

With straight needles A, cast on 60sts.
Work in k1, p1 rib for 5cm (2$^1/_4$in).
Change to straight needles B and cont in rib until work measures 50cm (20in) from beg. Change to straight needles A, and rib a further 5cm (2$^1/_4$in).
Cast off in rib.
Join back leg seam (see pp.36–37).

TOP TIP   *Continue the rib pattern to increase the height of the leg warmers.*

Essential information

SIZE To fit an adult female, shoe size UK 4-6

YARN

Debbie Bliss Baby Cashmerino 50g

A   B   C

A: 027 Denim x 3
B: 006 Candy pink x 2
C: 002 Apple x 2

NEEDLES

1 pair of 3.75mm (UK9/US5) needles

TENSION

25sts and 34 rows to 10cm (4in) over st st on
3.75mm (UK9/US5) needles

NOTIONS

1 stitch holder and spare needle
Stitch markers
Large-eyed needle

Striped knee-high socks

Adjust the length by knitting fewer or more rows after you shape the heel. Measure your legs first and work out the number of rows needed before you cast on.

Socks (make 2)

With yarn A, cast on 66sts.
ROW 1: K1, *k2, p2. Rep from * to last st, k1.
Rep until your work measures 3.5cm (1³/₈in).
ROWS 1-4: Join in yarn B and work 4 rows st st.
ROWS 5-8: Join in yarn C and work 4 rows st st.
ROWS 9-14: With yarn A, work 6 rows st st.
Cont to work 14 rows stripe sequence, until your work measures 45cm (17³/₄in) from cast on edge, finishing with a RS row.
NEXT ROW: P4, [p2tog, p5] x 8, p2tog, p4. (57sts)
Cont in stripe as set until work measures 61cm (23¹/₂in) from cast on edge.
Break off yarn.

Divide for heel

With RS facing, slip first 14sts onto RH needle, slip next 29sts onto a stitch holder for instep, slip rem 14sts onto a spare needle.
With WS facing, join yarn A to instep edge of 14sts on RH needle from previous row, p to end, turn spare needle around and p14 on spare needle. (28sts)
With yarn A, cont as follows:
NEXT ROW: K1, *k1, s1p, rep from * to last st, k1.
NEXT AND EVERY FOLL ALT ROW: P.
Rep these 2 rows x 9.

Turn heel

ROW 1: K15, skpo, k1, turn.
ROW 2: P4, p2tog, p1, turn.
ROW 3: K5, skpo, k1, turn.
ROW 4: P6, p2tog, p1, turn.
ROW 5: K7, skpo, k1, turn.
ROW 6: P8, p2tog, p1, turn.
ROW 7: K9, skpo, k1, turn.
ROW 8: P10, p2tog, p1, turn.
ROW 9: K11, skpo, k1, turn.

ROW 10: P12, p2tog, p1, turn.
ROW 11: K13, skpo, k1, turn.
ROW 12: P14, p2tog, p1. (16sts)
Break off yarn.
With RS facing, join yarn A to instep edge, pick up and k11 evenly along side edge of heel, k across 16sts of heel, then pick up and k11 along other side of heel. (38sts)
P 1 row.
ROW 1: K1, skpo, k to last 3sts, k2tog, k1. (36sts)
ROW 2 AND EVERY FOLL ALT ROW: P.
ROW 3: K.
ROW 4: As row 2.
Rep these 4 rows x 4. (28sts)
Cont in st st until work measures 18cm (7in) from back of heel, finishing with RS facing. (Length can be adjusted here, allowing 3.5cm (1³/₈in) for the toe shaping.)

**Shape toe

ROW 1: K1, skpo, k2, *p2, k2, rep from * to last 3sts, k2tog, k1. (26sts)
ROW 2: P2, *p2, k2, rep from * to last 4sts, p4.
ROW 3: K1, skpo, k1, *p2, k2, rep from * to last 6sts, p2, k1, k2tog, k1. (24sts)
ROW 4: P3, *k2, p2, rep from * to last 5sts, k2, p3.
Keeping continuity of rib as set, cont to dec 1st at each end of next and foll 4 alt rows. (14sts)
NEXT ROW: P2, *k2, p2, rep from * to end. **
Break off yarn and leave these 14sts on a spare needle.

Instep (RS facing)

Keeping continuity of stripes, k across 29sts on stitch holder, dec 1st at centre (28sts). (Place markers at each end of this row.)
Starting with a p row, work in st st and stripes

Each solid blue sole is seamed with a striped instep (see main picture, left) to form an enclosed foot.

as set until work measures the same as sole to toe shaping from markers.

Shape toe

With yarn A, work as for lower foot from ** to **. Placing RS of upper foot facing, cast off as follows: P2tog 1st from upper and lower foot, across all sts, casting off as each st is worked.

Making up

Join the upper and lower foot seams and back seam (see pp.36-37).

Essential information

SIZE To fit a child, aged 2–3 (4-5:6-7) years

YARN

Debbie Bliss Baby Cashmerino DK 50g

006 Candy pink x 5 (5:6)

NEEDLES

A: 1 pair of 2.75mm (UK12/US2) needles
B: 1 pair of 3.25mm (UK10/US3) needles

A

B

TENSION

25sts and 44 rows to 10cm (4in) over moss st on
3.25mm (UK10/US3) needles

NOTIONS

Large-eyed needle
5 (6:6) x 12mm (½in) buttons

Child's moss stitch cardigan

This v-neck cardigan for a little girl is given a soft, subtle texture using moss stitch, in a cashmere and wool blended yarn.

Back

With needles A, cast on 75 (83:91) sts.
K 3 rows.
Change to needles B.
MOSS ST ROW: K1, [p1, k1] to end.
Cont in moss st until back measures 16 (19:
22)cm (6^1/$_4$ (7^1/$_2$:9)in) from cast on edge,
ending with a WS row.

Shape armholes

Cast off 5sts at beg of next 2 rows. (65 (73:
81) sts)
Dec 1st at each end of next and 4 (5:6) foll RS
rows. (55 (61:67) sts)
Work straight until back measures 28 (32:
36)cm (11 (12^1/$_2$:14^1/$_4$)in) from cast on edge,
ending with a WS row.

Shape shoulders

Cast off 4sts at beg of next 4 rows and 5 (6:7)
sts at beg of foll 2 rows. (29 (33:37) sts)
Cast off.

Left front

With needles A, cast on 39 (43:47) sts.
K 3 rows.
Change to needles B.
ROW 1: [K1, p1] to last 3sts, k3.
ROW 2: K3, [p1, k1] to end.
These 2 rows form moss st with g st edging.
Cont in patt until front measures 16 (19:22)cm
(6^1/$_4$ (7^1/$_2$:9)in) from cast on edge, ending with
row 2.

Shape armhole and front neck

NEXT ROW: Cast off 5sts, patt to last 4sts, k2tog,
k2. (33 (37:41) sts)
NEXT ROW: K3, patt to end.

NEXT ROW: Work 2sts tog, patt to last 4sts,
k2tog, k2.
Rep the last 2 rows x 4 (5:6). (23 (25:27) sts)
Keeping armhole edge straight, cont to dec at neck
edge on every 4th row until 16 (17:18) sts rem.
Work straight until front measures same as back
to shoulder shaping, ending at armhole edge.

Shape shoulder

Cast off 4sts at beg of next and foll RS row.
Work 1 row.
NEXT ROW: Cast off 5 (6:7) sts, k to end. (3sts)
Cont on these 3sts until band fits halfway
across back neck.
Cast off. Mark position for buttons, the first on
4th row, the 5th (6th:6th) two rows below neck
shaping, and rem 3 (4:4) spaced evenly between.

Right front

With needles A cast on 39 (43:47) sts.
K 3 rows.
Change to needles B.
ROW 1 (BUTTONHOLE ROW): K1, k2tog, yrn, [p1,
k1] to end.
ROW 2: [K1, p1] to last 3sts, k3.
ROW 3: K3, [p1, k1] to end.
These 2 rows form moss st with g st edging.
Working buttonholes to match markers, cont in
patt until front measures 16 (19:22)cm (6^1/$_4$
(7^1/$_2$:9)in) from cast on edge, ending with row 2.

Shape armhole and front neck

NEXT ROW: K2, skpo, patt to end.
NEXT ROW: Cast off 5sts, patt to end. (33 (37:41)
sts)
NEXT ROW: K2, k2tog, patt to last 2sts, work 2tog.
NEXT ROW: [K1, p1] to last 3sts, k3.
Rep the last 2 rows x 4 (5:6). (23 (25:27) sts)

Keeping armhole edge straight cont to dec at neck
edge on every 4th row until 16 (17:18) sts rem.
Work straight until front measures same as back
to shoulder shaping, ending at armhole edge.

Shape shoulder

Cast off 4sts at beg of next and foll RS row.
Work 1 row.
NEXT ROW: Cast off 5 (6:7) sts, k to end. (3sts)
Cont on these 3sts until band fits halfway
across back neck. Cast off.

Sleeves (make 2)

With needles A, cast on 35 (39:43) sts.
K 3 rows.
Change to needles B.
MOSS ST ROW: K1, [p1, k1] to end.
Work a further 5 rows.
INC ROW: K1, M1, patt to last st, M1, k1.
Work 7 rows.
Rep the last 8 rows x 10 (11:12) and the inc row
again. (59 (65:71) sts)
Cont straight until sleeve measures 25 (28:
31)cm (9^3/$_4$ (11:12^1/$_4$)in) from cast on edge,
ending with a WS row.

Shape sleeve top

Cast off 5sts at beg of next 2 rows.
Dec 1st at each end of next and 8 (9.10) foll RS
rows. (31 (35:39) sts)
Cast off 2sts at beg of next 8 rows. Cast off.

Making up

Join the shoulder seams. Join the cast off edges
of the front bands, sew the band to the back of
the neck. Join the side and sleeve seams. Sew
in the sleeves. Sew on all of the buttons.

Essential information

SIZE To fit an adult male S (97cm/38in):
M (104cm/41in): L (112cm/44in): XL (119cm/47in)

YARN

Sublime Cashmere Merino Silk DK 50g

223 Latte x 7 (8:8:9)

NEEDLES

A: 1 pair of 3.75mm (UK9/US5) needles
B: 1 pair of 4mm (UK8/US6) needles

A

B

TENSION

22sts and 28 rows to 10cm (4in) over st st using
4mm (UK8/US6) needles

NOTIONS

2 stitch holders
Large-eyed needle

Men's sleeveless pullover

A timeless v-necked tank top knitted in stocking stitch with a 2x2 ribbed border. The yarn used here is a cashmere, merino wool and silk blended quality.

Back

With needles A, cast on 106 (118:130:142) sts.
RIB ROW 1. K2, [p2, k2] to end.
RIB ROW 2. P2, [k2, p2] to end
Rep the last 2 rows x 4 (5:6:7).
Change to needles B.
Beg with a k row cont in st st until back measures 44 (45:46:47)cm (17^1/$_2$ (17^3/$_4$:18:18^1/$_2$)in) from cast on edge, ending with a p row **.

Shape armholes

Cast off 10 (11:12:13) sts at beg of next 2 rows. (86 (96:106:116) sts)
NEXT ROW: K1, skpo, k to last 3sts, k2tog, k1.
NEXT ROW: P to end.
Rep the last 2 rows x 3 (4:5:6). (78 (86:94:102) sts)
Work straight until back measures 65 (67:69:71)cm (26 (26^1/$_4$:27:28)in) from cast on edge, ending with a WS row.

Shape shoulders

Cast off 8 (9:11:12) sts at beg of the next 2 rows and 9 (10:11:12) sts at beg of foll 2 rows.
Leave rem 44 (48:50:54) sts on a stitch holder.

Front

Work as given for Back to **. (106 (118:130:142) sts)

Shape armholes and neck

NEXT ROW: Cast off 10 (11:12:13) sts, k until there are 42 (47:52:57) sts on the needle, turn, and work on these sts for first side of neck shaping.
NEXT ROW: P to end.

NEXT ROW: K1, skpo, k to last 3sts, k2 tog, k1.
NEXT ROW: P to end.
Rep the last 2 rows x 3 (4:5:6). (34 (37:40:43) sts)
Keeping armhole edge straight cont to dec 1st at neck edge on every RS row until 17 (19:22:24) sts rem.
Cont straight until front measures the same as back to shoulder shaping, ending at armhole edge.

Shape shoulders

Cast off 8 (9:11:12) sts at beg of the next row.
Work 1 row.
Cast off rem 9 (10:11:12) sts.
With RS facing, slip next 2sts on a holder, rejoin yarn to rem sts, k to end.
NEXT ROW: Cast off 10 (11:12:13) sts, p to end. (42 (47:52:57) sts)
NEXT ROW: K1, skpo, k to last 3sts, k2 tog, k1.
NEXT ROW: P to end.
Rep the last 2 rows x 3 (4:5:6). (34 (37:40:43) sts)
Keeping armhole edge straight cont to dec 1st at neck edge on every RS row until 17 (19:22:24) sts rem.
Cont straight until front measures the same as back to shoulder shaping, ending at armhole edge.

Shape shoulders

Cast off 8 (9:11:12) sts at beg of the next row.
Work 1 row.
Cast off rem 9 (10:11:12) sts.

Neckband

Join right shoulder seam.
With RS facing and using needles A, pick up and k50 (52:56:58) sts evenly down left side of front neck, k2 from safety pin, pick up and k50 (52:54:56) sts evenly up RS of front neck, k44 (48:50:54) sts from back neck holder. (146 (154:162:170) sts)
1st and 4th sizes only
ROW 1: K2, [p2, k2] to end.
2nd and 3rd sizes only
ROW 1: P2, [k2, p2] to end.
All sizes
This row sets the rib patt.
ROW 2: Rib 49 (51:55:57), k2tog, skpo, rib to end.
ROW 3: Rib to end.
ROW 4: Rib 48 (50:54:56), k2tog, skpo, rib to end.
ROW 5: Rib to end.
ROW 6: Rib 47 (49:53:55), k2tog, skpo, rib to end.
ROW 7: Rib to end.
Cast off in rib, dec on this row as before.

Armbands

Join left shoulder seam and neckband.
With RS facing and using needles A, pick up and k118 (122:130:134) sts evenly around armhole edge.
ROW 1: K2, [p2, k2] to end.
ROW 2: P2, [k2, p2] to end.
These 2 rows set the rib patt.
Work a further 5 rows.
Cast off in rib.

Making up

Join side and armband seams (see pp.36–37 for more information)

Anytime shoulder bag

This bag is incredibly easy to knit because it is made up of one rectangle of knitted fabric worked in stocking stitch. We've included two options for the strap size, so you can wear it over your shoulder or across the body.

Essential information

SIZE 22 x 18cm (9 x 7in)

YARN

Rowan Belle Organic DK 50g

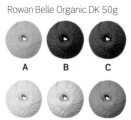

A: 026 Marina x 2   **B:** 021 Garnet x 2
C: 029 Dahlia x 1   **D:** 013 Moonflower x 1
E: 016 Cilantro x 1   **F:** 023 Bluebell x 1
Oddments of two different coloured yarns for marking (we've used red and black)

NEEDLES

A: 1 pair of 4.5mm (UK7/US7) needles
B: 1 pair of 5mm (UK6/US8) needles
C: 80cm (32in), 4.5mm (UK7/US7)
circular needle

TENSION

16sts and 23 rows to 10cm (4in) over st st using 5mm (UK6/US8) needles

NOTIONS

Large-eyed needle

Stripe pattern

6 rows in yarn F, 4 rows in A, 4 rows in C, 6 rows in B, 4 rows in A, 6 rows in F, 4 rows in A, 6 rows in D, 6 rows in E, 4 rows in yarn A. (50 rows in total)

Bag

Using needles A and yarn A, cast on 34sts. Starting with a k row, work 4 rows g st, ending with a WS row.
Set border and stripe patt
Change to needles B. Working as given for stripe patt (above), set border as follows:
ROW 1 (RS): K.
ROW 2: K3, p to last 3sts, k3.
Last 2 rows set border. Rep last 2 rows throughout. At same time, place black markers at each end of rows 56 and 65, and red markers at each end of rows 121 and 130. Cont in patt until work measures 80cm (31¹/₂in) from cast on edge, ending with a RS row.
Change to needles A; join in yarn A. Starting with a k row, work 3 rows g st. Cast off.
Darn in all ends and block as given on ballband.

Strap

Using needles C and yarn B, cast on 200sts for a short strap or child's bag, or 300sts for a long strap or adult's bag, placing black markers at 44th and 156th sts (or 256th st for longer strap). Starting with a k row (RS), work 4 rows g st. Break off B, join in C and work a further 4 rows g st. Cast off, placing black markers at 44th and 156th sts (256th st for longer strap). Darn in ends.

Making up

Lay main piece of bag flat with WS facing, align row ends of strap with bag row ends between red markers. Sew in place using backstitch (see p.37). Fold main bag piece around strap so that black markers on both pieces meet. Pin in place along bag row ends and strap cast on/cast off edges. Sew these side seams using backstitch. Darn in ends (see p.36).

Essential information

SIZE 32 x 38cm (12½ x 15in)

YARN

Rowan Colourscape Chunky 100g

447 Jungle x 2

NEEDLES

1 pair of 7mm (UK2/US n/a) needles

TENSION

(Before felting) 14sts and 28 rows to 10cm (4in)
over st st on 7mm (UK2/US n/a) needles

NOTIONS

20 (approx.) rhinestone studs

Felted tote bag

A roomy bag ideal for storing your yarn and needles, this project is worked in stocking stitch, then felted, and embellished with rhinestone studs. Refer to the felting instructions here, or follow the manufacturer's information on your ballband.

Cast on 50sts.

Starting with a k row, and working in st st, inc at both ends of 5th row. Work 9 rows without shaping. (52sts)

ROW 15 (RS): Inc in first st, k15, cast off 20sts, k15, inc in last st. (54sts)

ROW 16: P17, cast on 20sts, p to end.

Cont working in st st, inc at each end on 8th and every foll 10th row, until there are 66sts.

Work 19 rows without shaping.

Dec at each end of next and every foll 10th row until 54sts remain.

Work 8 rows without shaping.

NEXT ROW (WS): P17, cast off 20sts, p to end.

NEXT ROW: S1 k1 psso, k15, cast on 20sts, k to last 2sts, k2tog. (52sts)

Cont working in st st, dec on foll 10th row. Work 5 more rows without shaping. Cast off.

Fold work with WS facing you so that cast on and cast off edges meet. Join row ends using a long backstitch (see p.37), and felt the bag in the washing machine at 60°C (140°F), (see right). Stuff the felted bag with clean plastic bags to hold it in its pear shape and leave to dry. Add rhinestone studs on the bag, using the photograph as a guide.

How to felt your knitting

First, hand test the yarn to see if it will felt. Roll a 90cm (36in) long strand into a ball. Add a drop of detergent and rub it together for 2 minutes under hot running water. If the yarn clumps and is difficult to pull apart, it is a good candidate for test-felting. Next, knit and block a 10cm (4in) swatch. Submerge it in soapy hand-hot water. Squeeze and knead it gently, adding more hot water as required for up to 30 minutes. Rinse and squeeze out the water (do not wring) and roll in a towel. Pat the felt, right-side up, into a rectangle and leave to dry overnight. If the yarn has felted successfully, test a bigger swatch in a washing machine.

Preparing for test-felting

By test-felting a swatch of your yarn you can determine how much it will shrink, although felting is not an exact science. Washing machine agitation, water temperature, detergent type, and yarn fibre content, spin, and colour all vary.

Knit a swatch of stocking stitch at least 20cm (8in) square (accurate shrinkage measurements cannot be obtained with smaller swatches). Block the swatch carefully. If unblocked, the side edges will felt too thickly due to the curling.

Machine felting

Put a swatch in the washing machine along with a large towel (this increases the agitation). Add half the amount of detergent used for a full load. Wash at 40°C (104°F) for yarn that contains mohair, and 60°C (140°F) for 100 per cent wool yarns, using the full washing and spin cycle. Tug the washed swatch gently in both directions, lay it right-side up and pat into a rectangle. Leave to dry completely. If necessary, do more tests with new swatches, altering the temperature or the length of the wash cycle. Keep detailed records of tension, needle size, sizes of pre-felted and felted swatches, wash settings, and type and amount of detergent used.

Tips for felting

If you are trying felting for the first time, make several test swatches in different weights of yarn and felt them together in the same load. This way you can get a feel for the different thicknesses of knitted felt. When using highly contrasting colours, put a colour catcher sheet in the machine to absorb loose dye and prevent colours from running. Wool will fade slightly when felted, due to the high temperatures and the detergent, but this adds an attractive quality to the felt. Clean your washing machine after a felting load by wiping it out with a damp cloth to remove any stray fibres.

Mobile phone sock

Protect your phone with a knitted cover in a choice of three different colourways. Knitted in single rib, the sock includes a slim pocket to store a memory card or earphones. An ideal project for a beginner.

Essential information

SIZE 7 x 15cm (2¾ x 6in)

YARN

Patons Diploma Gold/Berroco Vintage DK 50g

A   **B**   **C**   **D**

A: 6220 Blue x 1/51190 Cerulean x 1 or
B: 6245 Plum x 1/5180 Dried plum x 1 or
C: 6125 Apple green x 1/5162 Envy x 1
D: 6142 White x 1/5100 Snow day x 1

NEEDLES

1 pair of 3.25mm (UK10/US3) needles

TENSION

30sts and 30 rows to 10cm (4in) over 1x1 rib on 3.25mm (UK10/US3) needles

NOTIONS

Large-eyed needle

Front and back (make 2)

In the colour of your choice (A, B, or C) cast on 21sts.
ROW 1: K1, [p1, k1] to end.
ROW 2: P1, [k1, p1] to end.
Rep these 2 rows to form 1x1 rib until your work measures 12cm (5in).
Work 1x1 rib, as above, 1 row in yarn D and 1 row in yarn A, B, or C x 4.
To halve the number of yarn ends when knitting single rows, cut off a piece of yarn about eight times the width of the work and knit the first row, starting from the middle of the strand. Do this again for the next colour, and then pick up the tail of the first yarn to knit the 3rd row. Continue in this way with a new strand of yarn introduced for every 2 rows of a colour instead of every row.
Cast off in stitch using yarn D.

Pocket

In yarn A, B, or C cast on 21sts.
ROW 1: K1, [p1, k1] to end.
ROW 2: P1, [k1, p1] to end.
Rep these 2 rows until your work measures 5cm (2in).
Work 1 row of 1x1 rib in yarn D and 1 row in yarn A, B, or C x 4.
Cast off in stitch using yarn D.

Making up

Lay the back piece RS up. Lay the pocket on top, RS down, lining up the cast on edges. Lay front piece on top with RS down, lining up the cast on edges. Backstitch (see p.37) down sides and across bottom. Turn through.

Protective cover This stitch is stretchy so the sock will fit most phones. Refer to p.30 for information on how to knit single ribbing.

Cuddly baby toys

Suitable for newborns to older babies, these stylized tiny cot toys are quick to knit. The patterns include stocking stitch and garter stitch with embroidered detailing.

Essential information

SIZE 14.5 x 6.5cm (6 x 2½in) approx.

YARN

Sublime Baby Cashmere Merino Silk DK 50g

A   **B**   **C**

A: 278 Muffin x 1   **B:** 03 Vanilla x 1
C: 124 Splash x 1
Scrap of yarn for embroidery (we've used 051 Button)

NEEDLES

A: 1 pair of 3.25mm (UK10/US3) needles
B: 1 pair of 4mm (UK8/US6) needles

———————————————————— A
———————————————————— B

TENSION

22sts and 28 rows to 10cm (4in) over st st on 4mm (UK8/US6) needles

NOTIONS

Large-eyed needle
Polyester toy filling
Water-soluble pen
Spray bottle (optional)

Knitted lamb toy

The body and head are knitted together from the base to the top of the head.

Body and head (make 2)

Using needles A and yarn A, cast on 18sts.
K 34 rows.
Break yarn and join yarn B.
Work 10 rows in st st.
NEXT ROW: K2, k2tog, k to last 4sts, ssk, k2. (16sts)
NEXT ROW: P2tog, p to last 2sts, p2tog. (14sts)
Rep last 2 rows once more. (10sts)
Cast off.

Ears (make 2)

Using needles A and yarn B, cast on 10sts.
ROW 1: P.
ROW 2: K1, k2tog, k4, ssk, k1. (8sts)
ROW 3: P2tog, p4, p2tog. (6sts)
ROW 4: K1, k2tog, ssk, k1. (4sts)
ROW 5: [P2tog] x 2. (2sts)
ROW 6: K2tog. (1st)
Break yarn and pull through rem st.

Forelock

Using needles B and yarn A, cast on 5sts.
ROW 1: Inc 1st, k2, inc 1st, k1. (7sts)
K 2 rows.
NEXT ROW: K2tog, k3, ssk. (5sts)
Cast off.

Making up

Join the side seams and top seam of the lamb using mattress stitch (see p.37) and matching yarns. Make sure all yarn tails are secure and on the inside of your toy. Stuff fairly lightly with toy filling. Sew the lower edge using mattress stitch. Fold the ears in half lengthways with RS on the outside. Oversew the seam close to the edge. Oversew the ears in place so that the seams are at the front. Secure the forelock in place by working a circle of running stitch around the edge. Using the photograph as a guide, draw on the lamb's features using the water-soluble pen. Work French knots for the eyes using an oddment of yarn and a large-eyed needle. Embroider three straight stitches in a "Y" shape for the nose and mouth. Spray the toy lightly with water to remove the pen marks and leave to dry.

TOP TIP   *Give the toys different expressions by varying your embroidery.*

Knitted kitten toy

The body and head are knitted together from the base to the top of the head.

Body and head (make 2)

Cast on 18sts in yarn C.

K 34 rows.

Break yarn and join yarn A.

Work 12 rows in st st.

ROW 47: K8, cast off 2sts, k to end.

ROW 48: P8, turn and work on these 8sts only, leaving rem sts on needle.

ROW 49: K1, k2tog, k to end. (7sts)

ROW 50: P.

Rep last 2 rows x 2. (5sts)

ROW 55: K1, k2tog, k2. (4sts)

ROW 56: [P2tog] x 2. (2sts)

ROW 57: K2tog. (1st)

Break yarn and pull through rem st.

Rejoin yarn to rem sts on WS of work.

ROW 58: P.

ROW 59: K to last 3sts, ssk, k1. (7sts)

ROW 60: P.

Rep last 2 rows x 2. (5sts)

ROW 65: K2, ssk, k1. (4sts)

ROW 66: [P2tog] x 2. (2sts)

ROW 67: Ssk. (1st)

Break yarn and pull through rem st.

Making up

Join the side seams using mattress stitch (see p.37) and matching yarns. Turn the kitten inside out and oversew round the ears. Turn the kitten RS out again. Make sure all yarn tails are secure and on the inside of your toy. Stuff with polyester toy filling. Sew the lower edge closed. Using the photograph as a guide, draw on the kitten's features using the water-soluble pen. Embroider the features in backstitch (see p.37), using an oddment of yarn and a large-eyed needle. Spray the toy lightly with water to remove the pen marks and leave to dry.

Essential information

SIZE 12 x 12cm (5 x 5in)

YARN

Debbie Bliss Rialto DK 50g

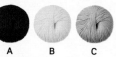

A   B   C

A: 12 Scarlet x 1
B: 01 White x 1
C: 42 Pink x 1

NEEDLES

1 pair of 3.75mm (UK9/US5) needles

TENSION

26sts and 30 rows to 10cm (4in) over st st on
3.75mm (UK9/US5) needles

NOTIONS

Large-eyed needle
Polyester toy stuffing
90cm (35in) x 6mm (¼in)-wide red ribbon
Sewing needle and red sewing thread
3 x 1cm (½in) mother-of-pearl buttons

Heart sachets

A trio of hanging hearts that sport knitted and embroidered motifs.

Red heart (make 2)

With yarn A, cast on 3sts.
K 1 row and p 1 row.
Now shape sides as follows:

ROW 1: K1, yon, k1, yon, k1.

ROW 2: P1, yrn, p into back of yon on previous row, p1, p into back of yon on previous row, yrn, p1.

ROW 3: K1, yon, k into back of yrn on previous row, k3, k into back of yrn on previous row, yon, k1.

ROW 4: P1, yrn, p into back of yon on previous row, p5, p into back of yon on previous row, yrn, p1.

ROW 5: K1, yon, k into back of yrn on previous row, k to last 2sts, k into back of yrn on previous row, yon, k1.

ROW 6: P1, yrn, p into back of yon on previous row, p to last 2sts, p into back of yon on previous row, yrn, p1.

Rep the last 2 rows until there are 35sts, ending with a p row. *

Cont in st st, beg with a k row, work 20 rows straight.

**Shape top.

NEXT ROW: K17, turn and cont on these sts only for first side.
Now dec 1st at both ends of next 5 rows. (7sts)
Cast off.
With RS of work facing, rejoin yarn to rem sts.
K2tog and then k to end.
Dec 1st at both ends of next 5 rows. (7sts)
Cast off.
Following Chart 1, below left, and using yarn B, cross-stitch a heart in the centre of both sides.

Pink heart (make 2)

Using yarn C, work as for Red Heart until there are 31sts, ending with a p row. **Cont to shape sides as set until there are 35sts, at the same time now work in patt from Chart 2, below centre.** Odd numbers are RS rows and read from right to left, even numbered rows are WS rows and read from left to right. Use a separate ball of yarn for each area of colour, twisting yarns tog when joining colours to avoid a hole from forming. When chart is complete, work a further 6 rows st st using yarn C only.
Complete as given for Red Heart from ** to end.

White heart (make 2)

Using yarn B, work as for Red Heart to *.
Following Chart 3, below right, work 14 rows in Fair Isle patt.
When chart is complete, work a further 6 rows st st using yarn B only.
Complete as given for Red Heart from ** to end.

Making up

Place front and back together with RS facing and stitch around outer edges, leaving a small opening in one straight edge. Turn RS out. Stuff the hearts and stitch closed. Cut a length of ribbon 30cm (12in) long and sew it to the top of the front with matching thread. Sew on one button to cover the raw ends of the ribbon.

Chart 1

Chart 2

Chart 3

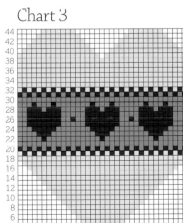

KEY

⬛	Scarlet
⬜	White
🟪	Pink

Index

Acknowledgments

Dorling Kindersley UK would like to thank the following people for their hard work and contributions towards *Classic Knits*:

Knitting consultant Dr Vikki Haffenden
Pattern checker Carol Ibbetson
Proofreader Angela Baynham
Indexer Marie Lorimer
Editorial assistance Becky Alexander, Kathryn Meeker
Yarn photographer in India Deepak Aggarwal
Location for photography 1st Option
Props George & Beth, Backgrounds

Knitting designers Caroline Birkett, Shirley Bradford, Sian Brown, Tessa Dennison, Lara Evans, Julie Ferguson, Vikki Haffenden, Amanda Jones.

Knitters Ruth Bridgeman, Pauline Buck, Grace Coombs, Sally Cuthbert, Ursula Doherty, Joan Doyle, Eva Hallas, Jill Houghton, Dolly Howes, Karen Howie, Brenda Jennings, Ann McFaull, Elaine Morris, Daphne Moyce, Mrs Parsons, Doreen Payne, Karen Tattersall, Jane Wales, Brenda Willows.

Yarn manufacturers and distributors for supplying yarn for the projects Artesano Ltd, Coats Crafts UK, Designer Yarns, Kelbourne Woolens, King Cole Ltd, Rico Design, Sirdar Yarns, Sublime Yarns, Texere Yarns Ltd for providing yarn for the projects.

Many thanks to Ria Holland for design assistance on the Easy Craft Series.